Celtic Sexuality

Celtic Sexuality

Power, Paradigms and Passion

Peter Cherici

Duckworth

First published in the USA in 1994
by The Tyrone Press

First published in the UK in 1995 by
Gerald Duckworth & Co. Ltd.
The Old Piano Factory
48 Hoxton Square, London N1 6PB
Tel: 0171 729 5986
Fax: 0171 729 0015

A catalogue record for this book is available
from the British Library

ISBN 0 7156 2688 4

Typeset by Ray Davies
Printed in Great Britain by
Redwood Books Ltd, Trowbridge

Contents

Plates

between pages 96 and 97

A female dancing figure, 3rd Century AD (Musée Archéologique, Orléans)

Gallo-Roman representation of motherhood (Musée Vertillum, Burgundy)

The sheela-na-gig (Kilpeck, Herefordshire)

St Brigid

Queen Maev

Cuchulain (Dublin Post Office)

The Curse of Macha

Celtic women who dwelt under the sea

The children of Lir

Epona, the horse goddess

Reconstruction of the grave of a Celtic noblewoman

Boudica and her daughters (National Museum of Wales)

Queen Guinevere (Tate Gallery, London)

For Coleen O'Brien Cherici

1

Sexual Transitions

In an isolated village of County Mayo, a group of modern sociologists discovered that most of the local men did not understand the capacity of women to enjoy an orgasm. When these Irish men bedded an occasional female tourist, they were surprised by her squirming, by her active participation in the pursuit of sexual pleasure. The village women displayed no similar ardour, refusing to explore sexual activities beyond the grudging acceptance of male penetration. Upon further investigation, the researchers concluded that the gulf in sexual communication between men and women in modern rural Ireland was largely due to the repressive influence of the Catholic Church. They felt that conservative priests who immigrated to Ireland after the French Revolution helped to create attitudes biased against sexual expression.[1] While these researchers were wise to examine the past to discover the roots of modern sexual practices, they did not search far enough into history. Many of the ideas shaping current Irish sexual viewpoints emerged long before the French Revolution, transmitted from generation to generation by the institutions of society. In part, how the men and women of modern rural Mayo viewed the role of sexuality in their lives stemmed from the experiences and values of the Celts who lived in Ireland and Britain more than a millennium ago.

The sexual customs of the ancient Celts were far different from the practices of their modern descendants. But their sexual beliefs were not static, flowing steadily from parent to child in an unbroken stream linking the past with the present. Celtic ideals about sexual behaviour varied from time to time and place to place, responding to changes in political, religious, and scientific concepts. As part of the fundamental way the Celts viewed themselves and the world, sexuality was directly related to the belief system embodied in the basic institutions of their society. As long as family, government and religion remained stable, sexual beliefs were relatively constant. But when dramatic events demonstrated shortcomings in the ability of the traditional institutions to meet extreme challenges to the Celtic way of life, people began to question the validity of their institutions and paradigms. This sometimes caused Celtic society to destabilize as people searched for innovative solutions to new and unusual problems. During troubled times, perspectives of government, religion and law shifted, causing a restructuring of the basic Celtic viewpoints and institutions. And since sexuality could not be isolated from the other components of Celtic society, sexual ideas had to redefine themselves to conform to the shifting world view mandated by change. As a result, children could brand as perversion the common bedroom practices of their parents.

In the northern islands of Britain and Ireland where Celtic society survived intact after the collapse of the Roman Empire, several major events occurred to destabilize Celtic society. In the fifth century AD, Christianity ignited religious fever seldom seen before. In the sixth century AD, the Saxon conquest of Britain decimated Celtic armies and drove refugees into the lands to the west. In the twelfth century AD, the Anglo-Norman invasion of Ireland marked the beginning of the end of Celtic society. In response to each of these cultural crises, the Celts altered the way they viewed themselves and the world, including their sexual beliefs.

The spread of Christianity may have had the most impact on the sexual customs and practices of the Celts. But at first, the new religion had little influence on the traditional Celtic way of life. Christian and druid beliefs merged to form a hybrid system known as Celtic Christianity, giving the new faith a high level of legitimacy among the Celts. Modelled on local political institutions, the Celtic 'Church' was composed of a decentralized group of hermits, abbots, and secular priests who relied upon private interpretation of scripture. The clergy created no hierarchy to rival the rigid structure established by the Bishop of Rome, the leader of the Roman version of Christianity.[2] In its infancy, Celtic Christianity developed independently from mainland Europe, looking to native custom to supplement scripture. They were not acquainted with the Bishop of Rome's claims of absolute authority over all Christians.[3]

But even in its local form, the doctrines of Christianity required a complete revamping of the way the Celts viewed themselves and the universe. Christian philosophy introduced a duality of mind and spirit into the Celtic culture, a split between the body and the intellect.[4] The Christian writings of Augustine, Jerome, and other Mediterranean based scholars divorced reason from passion, severing the mind from the flesh. Unlike the druid Celts, the Christians did not view themselves as integrated beings linked harmoniously to the world around them. Instead, they saw themselves as fragmented creatures with a spirit separate from nature, doomed to constantly war with the urges of their own bodies.

This duality had a profound effect on the Celtic approach to sexuality. Before the arrival of Christianity, a Celtic sexual relationship was a comfortable experience, a pleasurable communication between lovers essential for continued fertility. Sexuality was a fundamental part of existence, intertwined with war, spirituality, and the many other aspects of the human adventure. But Christianity gradually introduced the viewpoint that sexuality should not be fully integrated with human existence. Instead, sexual desire should be isolated, controlled, and ultimately conquered.

As a source of potential pleasure, the Christians of the time shunned sexual relations unless the object of the act was to create children. And even during this single allowed instance of permissible sex, enjoyment was forbidden. If age or disease made procreation impossible for a married couple, they were advised to live chastely together as brother and sister.[5] Nowhere did early Christian doctrine recognize sex as an expression of love between two people.

The Christians also taught the Celts to link sexual behaviour with morality. The nature of the relationship, the form of the activity, and the purpose behind it all had to be weighed on an ethical scale. It was an all or none proposition. The good achieved through procreation had to overbalance the spiritual damage caused by sexual gratification. The Celts who adopted the new sexual viewpoints of the Christians believed the change was evolutionary, demonstrating a passage into a higher state of enlightenment. They condemned the practices of their ancestors, creating a conflict with those who did not share their sexual beliefs.

Because the sexuality of the Celts was closely related with the other institutions of their society, sexual behaviour exerted an influence on events beyond the bed chamber. Sexual desire caused fleets to sail, armies to march, and monarchs to lose their crowns. Concepts about proper sexual conduct influenced philosophy, medicine, and religion. Sexuality charged the Celtic environment in subtle ways not always apparent to the men and women who responded instinctively to their passions and impulses.

But the Celtic Christians were not particularly adept at recognizing and exploiting the interplay of sexuality with the other institutions of their society. They did not dispatch men and women to use sexual guile to entice pagan monarchs into Christian conversion. If a powerful ruler was promiscuous, they chastised the behaviour publicly. Rarely did they use a moderate approach when confronted by sexual practices varying from Christian doctrine.

In contrast, the Roman Christian rivals of the Celtic Christians appeared to appreciate the political uses of sexuality. The development of many of the Christian sexual doctrines coincided with the expansion of the political and ecclesiastical power of the Bishop of Rome. During the last years of the Roman Empire, the Christians enjoyed theological supremacy. All other religious expressions were forbidden by civil law. But the collapse of the Empire diminished the political power of the Christians and the Bishops of Rome. The invading Goths, Visigoths, Franks, and Lombards were either pagan or followed the Arian sect of Christianity which did not recognize the primacy of Rome. It took several centuries for the Bishops of Rome to regain the stature they once enjoyed under the Caesars. First in Italy, then in France and Spain, the Bishops of Rome gradually re-established both temporal and ecclesiastical power.[6]

While there is no clear evidence that the Bishops of Rome viewed sexuality as a tool to enhance their power, they did enjoy the political benefit resulting from sexual liaisons. Many Christian women married pagan kings, converting them to the Roman Christian sect. When monarchs were not well disposed towards Roman Christian activity, their sexual practices provided a basis for censure. Pagans who did not submit to the authority of the Bishop of Rome were condemned as licentious and immoral. Sexual behaviour also helped to quell internal dissent within the Roman Christian clergy since few priests and monks could withstand intimate scrutiny.

This did not mean that the Christian doctrines limiting sexual expression were created with specific political uses in mind. The anti-pleasure bias crept into Christian thought from numerous external sources such as Gnosticism, Judaism, and Manicheanism. But once the rules controlling sexuality were in place, they proved eminently useful in developing and maintaining power. With banishment from the community as a potential punishment, few Christians were brave enough to challenge the established order. As a result, the Christian clergy established an enduring tradition which permitted sworn celibates to dictate the limits of sexuality to their followers.

When confronted with the sexual ethic developed by the Roman Christians, the customs and practices of the Celts struggled to survive. But the Saxon conquest of most of Britain added to the stress threatening to destabilize Celtic society. Within the course of a century, the military success of the invaders completely destroyed Celtic culture in southern Britain. After their conversion to the Roman Christian faith, the Saxons continued their conflict with the Celts until their descendants overwhelmed all of Ireland and Scotland more than a millennium later.

The failure of traditional Celtic political, military, and religious institutions to adequately deal with the Saxon menace helped to accelerate the process of change in sexual practice. People began to examine the ancient beliefs and search for innovative solutions to new problems. When they adopted Christianity to provide the answers to their questions, the Christian world view demanded a revolution in sexual outlook.

The Celtic version of Christianity was a transitional phase in the sexual history of the Celts. The native Christian sect was neither as liberal as the druids nor as repressively controlling as their Roman Christian rivals. Initially, only the ascetics behind monastery walls were subject to the full range of Christian sexual regulation. And the Celts who remained pagan were largely indifferent to Christian sexual beliefs.

But the Roman Christians took exception to most of the Celtic Christian practices which they viewed as unacceptable laxness. As the power of the Bishop of Rome expanded to encompass the British Isles, a confrontation was inevitable between the two Christian sects. By allying with the political enemies of the Celts, the Roman Christians profited from the rising fortune of the Saxons. At the Synod of Whitby in 664 AD, the Roman sect gained prestige when the Saxon king of Northumbria decided to restrict Celtic Christian practices in his domain. During the following centuries, the Celtic Christians slowly lost ground in their doctrinal battle with the Bishop of Rome.

The Anglo-Norman invasion of Ireland in 1169 AD was another destabilizing event for the Celts. The Bishop of Rome encouraged this military action with the Bull Laudabiliter which gave leave to the English King to enter Ireland to eliminate the lingering deviations from Roman dogma in the remote Celtic lands.[7] The invasion completed the process of religious conquest, eventually destroying the last strongholds of the Celtic Christians. And it set in motion a conflict between the Celts and the English which would result in the annihilation of Celtic society in Ireland four centuries later.

The gradual change of Celtic sexual attitudes from the ancient to the modern was a lengthy and complex process filled with contradiction. The introduction of Christianity, the Saxon invasion of Britain, and the English conquest of Ireland all had a dramatic impact on Celtic society, institutions and beliefs. When faced with a major crisis, Celtic paradigms changed to accommodate the events challenging their way of life. And people would embrace new perceptions of sexuality. Afterwards, paradox often resulted as traditional practices imperfectly fused with new ideas. But eventually, Celtic society found itself unable to compete politically, militarily, and philosophically with the English and the Roman Christians. Ultimately, the forces demanding sexual conformity with mainstream European thought overwhelmed them.

2

The Land of Innocence

Before the arrival of Christianity in Ireland, bards described the land as female, identifying it with the Goddesses Banba, Fótla, and Ériu. They called the twin hills rising from the rocky soil of Kerry the Paps of Anu, the breasts of the Mother Goddess. And in their poems, they likened the narrow valleys and ravines to the vulva of the fertile earth.[1]

While the feminine naming of the land recognized the pivotal role of fertility to an agricultural society, it also reflected the relaxed view of Celts towards their own sexuality. In this countryside where mountains were breasts and valleys were vulvae, the imagery evoked by their surroundings urged men and women to make love freely, without guilt. Sexual activity was a normal human function, perhaps even an act of worship in a culture valuing fertility. And legitimate erotic encounters were not limited to pursuit of pleasure and reproduction. Sexual liaisons between people were acceptable means to acquire property, status or political advancement.

Roman historians were the first to comment on Celtic sexual habits. They found their neighbours in Gaul and Britain promiscuous, unable to restrain their unbridled appetites. With disdain, they noted the existence of polygamous and polyandrous marriages.[2] But observers like Julius Caesar and Cassius Dio came from a patriarchal society with rigid rules governing the behaviour of women and the permitted relationships between the genders. In addition, Romans believed themselves superior in all respects to the outland barbarians. And they never considered that Celtic sexual behaviour might be merely different, not inherently inferior.

The Roman social system recognized only one form of monogamous marriage, a strict union under the firm authority of the husband. Despite the popular notion that Romans of both sexes were wantonly lascivious, female adultery was severely punished and premarital female promiscuity was discouraged. Augustus Caesar went as far as to banish his daughter, Julia, for her flagrant infidelities to her husband. Men had more freedom to pursue sexual adventures beyond home and hearth by visiting coarse, quasi-legal brothels staffed by slaves of both sexes and females of lower status. Eventually, more sophisticated forms of sexual expression developed in the later years of the Empire, resulting in the notorious excesses of the Imperial Court.[3]

In contrast, the Irish and Welsh social systems allowed several categories of marriage. They also gave legal status to many types of non-marriage unions. In all officially recognized relationships, women retained a high degree of independence, controlling property and their choice of extramarital lovers.[4] To the sexually conservative Romans, these Celtic 'marriages' would indeed seem libertine.

As additional evidence of promiscuity, the Romans cited the behaviour of the Celtic women at the siege of Sergovia. From the ramparts of the beleaguered city, scores of women bared their breasts as an act of entreaty to the Roman army below. Some even offered their bodies for the pleasure of the soldiers if the invaders would spare the city.[5] To the Romans, these acts were little better than prostitution. But the Celtic women believed they were placing a burden of shame upon the Romans for forcing them to barter their sexuality in exchange for life. Since the Celts did not use writing, any rebuttal they might have made to the Roman criticism of their sexual behaviour was not recorded. But they did leave behind a substantial body of orally transmitted myths which reveal the preChristian attitudes of the Celts toward their own sexuality. Since these myths largely reflect the thoughts and perceptions of the people who created them, they are more valuable than the observations of Roman outsiders as a source of information concerning Celtic sexual viewpoints. In dramatic form, they outline Celtic ideas regarding sex, love, and the intimate relationships between people.

In Celtic society, bards were charged with preserving the words of the myths. To help the people make sense of the great events of their lives, to explain the meaning of birth, death, and war, the bards would recite appropriate excerpts. They used memory alone to perpetuate the myths, an art requiring many years of specialized training. And since the myths were living parables, it is reasonable to assume that bards would alter the words over time to make them more effective for the circumstances of a particular audience. While it is impossible to know with certainty, the mythic words spoken by bards at the time of the Roman invasion of Britain probably varied from the mythic words spoken four hundred years later.

When writing was introduced in Britain and Ireland by the Christians, the Celtic monks respected their heritage enough to record the oral tradition of the bards. On these islands, distant from the political and religious centres of the Mediterranean, a vast body of Celtic myth survived into historical times. Unfortunately, the Christian monks of Gaul and Galatia did not follow the example of their cousins in Britain and Ireland. No Celtic mythological cycles survive intact from Continental Europe, probably due to centuries of suppression of the druids by the Roman Empire followed by the hostility to secular knowledge displayed by Roman Christians.

The Celtic Christians of Ireland and Britain did not feel threatened by learning that did not relate directly to religion. They believed that all forms of knowledge complemented Christianity, leading ultimately to a higher spirituality. This viewpoint sharply differed from the doctrine of the Roman Christians who discouraged the use of literacy to explore profane subjects.[6] But the Celtic monks lived far from Rome, answering only to the local abbots who they elected to administer their monasteries. As a result, they not only recorded the mythology of their ancestors, but they included many passages conflicting directly with Christian teachings. Only occasionally did they succumb to the temptation to embellish the myths with Christian doctrine or outcomes.[7] To justify their labour involving the pagan and profane, the monks accepted the myths as historical chronicles. Gradually, the gods and goddesses of the pre-Christian world lost their divinity and became the heroes and heroines of a lost age.

The Yellow Plague of 663-667 AD provided a further stimulus to chronicle the myths of the past. Confronted with widespread sickness and death, the monks felt compelled to commit their heritage to paper, fearing that the memory might be lost to succeeding generations.[8] And perhaps due to haste, perhaps as a form of monastic pornography, the monks failed to censor passages of the myths dealing with sexuality.

*

In the court of King Conchobhar of Ulster, CúChulain was the ideal man. Strong, handsome, and intelligent, he easily attracted the attention of women. And this created a disturbing situation for the other men of Conchobhar's court. They never knew if they would return home to find CúChulain pleasuring their wives or daughters. So Conchobhar searched the land to find a mate worthy of CúChulain, theorizing that if CúChulain's sexual needs were satisfied by a wife, he would be less likely to trouble other women.

At the king's urging, CúChulain courted Emer. During their first meeting, they spoke of sex freely and easily. Glancing at Emer's breasts, CúChulain said, 'I see a sweet country. I could rest my weapon there.'[9] But Emer refused to make love with CúChulain until he performed a number of exploits. CúChulain's ready compliance with Emer's conditions recognized the Celtic custom of female choice of sexual partners and granted her control over their future sexual union.

But the relationship between CúChulain and Emer also displayed the underlying conflict between the genders found in Celtic myth. Men and women jousted with each other for supremacy. Women identified with the fruitful earth, with human passions and renewal of life. In direct opposition, men clung to the gods of the sky, to the deities of reason who were remote from reproduction. Yet sexuality remained a common ground of communication between the genders, a need recognized by both men and women.

Generally, women in Celtic myth enjoyed full control of their sexuality, dispensing their favours as they saw fit. Men, however, frequently attempted to harness female sexuality through the forceful subjugation of passion by reason. In part, this reflected the position of women in Celtic society. They did not enjoy full equality with men. But neither was Celtic society a patriarchy. Women could contract, bear arms, become druids, and engage in politics. If they tired of a husband, they could divorce. And for some men, particularly those enmeshed by the male ethics of a warrior sodality, the sexual and reproductive freedom of women was an intolerable situation.

The early myth of Cessair focused on the threat to males posed by female sexuality. According to the *Book of Invasions*, she was the first inhabitant of Ireland. She arrived with three men and fifty women. Eventually, two of the men died, drained of their life force by an excess of sexual liaisons with the women. The remaining man fled, hiding from the demands of his female companions. And the women died, frustrated by their inability to realize the promise of their latent fertility.[10]

To make the land prosper, union between male and female was necessary. But the sexual requirements of the female were great and potentially deadly. The myth of Cessair warned men to be wary of women.

The next mythic group to inhabit Ireland was led by a man, Partholon. When he was away on a hunt, his wife had a sexual fling with Toba. After Partholon returned home, he discovered his wife's indiscretion and killed her lapdog out of jealousy. She responded:

> Honey with a woman, milk with a cat,
> food with one generous, meat with a child,
> a wright within and edged tool,
> one before one, 'tis a great risk.[11]

With this statement, Partholon's wife asserted her right to

control her own sexuality. She also defined the male duty to impregnate the female or risk loss of the opportunity to enjoy her favours. The female sexual needs were indifferent to the rules of monogamous marriage, scorning any attempt by males to control her passion with arbitrary regulations. Infidelity was not the fault of the wife, but the fault of the husband for leaving her sexual and reproductive urges unfulfilled.

Eventually, the Tuatha Dé Danaan came to Ireland, the people of the goddess Danu. Descending from the sky in a cloud of mist, they were a race of beings both beautiful and wise, a people of godlike abilities. In two great battles, they defeated the Fomorians, the primitive inhabitants of the land who identified closely with the female principles of earth and sea.

The Tuatha Dé Danaan served to define the male and female role functions in ancient Irish society, exercising patronage over the tasks important to an agricultural people. For example, Dian Cécht was a master physician and the Dagda was an enchanting musician. They were all sexually active, but some displayed a greater appetite than others. Under similar names, some of the characters of the Tuatha Dé Danaan also appeared in Welsh myth.

The Mórrígán was the patroness of war and the battle slain. She had three aspects, like most of the female Tuatha Dé Danaan. She was known not only as the Mórrígán, but also as Nemain the Venomous and Badb the Skald Crow. Generally, a male who sought her assistance in battle had to sleep with her beforehand. At the second battle against the Fomorians, the Dagda traded sex with her in return for the death of his enemy, Indech. But if the Mórrígán offered her sexual favours and was refused, she would become a most fearsome enemy.

Angus óg was another of the Tuatha Dé Danaan who was sexually precocious. But he added a dimension of love to his sexual liaisons, never coupling with a woman for pleasure or power alone. He went to great lengths to win the affections and sexual attentions of females, recognizing the need of men and women to be in a partnership where neither gender held dominance over the other.

As mortals gained ascendancy in the land, the Tuatha Dé

Danaan retired to the Otherworld. Occasionally, they sallied forth into the realm of the living to influence human events or enjoy a sexual encounter. Sometimes, mortals entered the Otherworld and found themselves subject to physical laws beyond their comprehension. And the bards sang of the Tuatha Dé Danaan, holding up their exploits as an example for all Celts to imitate.

The mythological cycles portrayed sexuality as a pleasurable necessity to be treated with caution. But for the male warrior, surrounded by gruff comrades and trophies of the hunt, sexuality was seen as a potential menace. The moment of male and female union was beyond the control of the warrior, a moment when he was vulnerable before woman, exposed to the mysteries of fertility. And to fortify himself against his own fears, CúChulain spoke of subjugating the fair country between Emer's breasts by resting his 'weapon', his penis, in that land.

Warrior sodalities were not an exclusively Celtic phenomenon. They appeared in many cultures tracing their origins to the Indo-European invasions of Europe, reflecting a tradition continuing to the present day. They consisted of a group of men, sworn to battle in the service of a leader or an ideal. In war and sometimes in peace, a berserker frenzy could help them achieve their goals. An internal code governed the behaviour of the sodality and the members displayed an almost religious devotion to the standards of conduct. They operated beyond the conventional rules of society. Women were never admitted to the ranks of the sodality and desire for their company was scorned as a sign of weakness.[12]

In Celtic myth, CúChulain was the exemplary member of a warrior sodality. He was devoted to the arts of war, a fighting man beyond compare. He owed his allegiance to Conchobhar, King of Ulster. And with his comrades, he performed great deeds of valour, battling the enemies of his leader.

As such an outstanding member of a male warrior sodality, CúChulain was the perfect candidate to subdue the wild and dangerous sexuality of the female. He did not engage in voluntary sexual relations unless he exercised complete domination over his partner. The only time he relinquished control to a woman occurred when his leader commanded him to woo Emer, the lady who placed conditions on their marriage. If he were not acting under royal orders, he probably would not have adhered to the rituals of courtship demanded by Emer.

After leaving Emer to perform the tasks set by her, CúChulain went to the island of the woman warrior Scáthach. By placing his sword between her breasts, he forced her to grant her daughter to warm his bed. In a later combat to defend Scáthach's realm, he subdued the female battle leader Aife and also brought her to his bed. Both of these sexual liaisons focused on the use of force to subjugate a dangerous female.[13]

After returning to Conchobhar's court, CúChulain became involved in a war between Ulster and Connaught over possession of a great bull that Queen Maev of Connaught stole for her own herd. Maev was a flamboyant woman, a leader in politics and on the field of battle. She was totally in control of her sexuality. She boasted to her husband that she 'never had one man without another waiting in his shadow.'[14] She engaged in countless sexual adventures, presumably for pleasure and excitement. But she rarely failed to use her sexuality to gain some political advantage over her lovers.

Maev represented Celtic female sexuality at its fullest expansion. CúChulain and the warrior sodality of Ulster recoiled from her in horror. She was a woman beyond their power to harness, a wild and malevolent force able to steal their cattle with seeming impunity. But of all the warriors of Ulster, only CúChulain was able to stand against her.

Many years before the war against Maev, King Conchobhar had forced the pregnant woman Macha to race against his horses due to a thoughtless boast by her husband. At the end of the race, Macha gave birth to twins. And in her labour pains, she cursed the warriors of Ulster, exclaiming, 'At the hour of your greatest need you also will be weakened by the pangs of childbirth!'[15] As a result of Macha's malediction, Queen Maev's attempted invasion of Ulster triggered a pain similar to childbirth throughout King Conchobhar's warrior sodality. Only CúChulain was spared since he was not born in Ulster.

Macha's curse added to the fear and loathing of the male warriors against women. Not only was their enemy led onto the field of battle by a woman, but another woman mysteriously enfeebled them with a distress specific only to females. But in their weakened state, Conchobhar's troops could do nothing to retaliate. They were doomed to watch helplessly as CúChulain alone faced the army of Queen Maev, guarding the ford through which the enemy must pass.

When Maev sent her daughter Finnabair to tempt CúChulain away from his position at the ford with an offer of sex, he responding by thrusting a pillar of stone 'under her cloak and tunic'.[16] This appeared to indicate that he impaled Finnabair through her vagina, although she survived to eventually become CúChulain's lover. And this act violently asserted the contempt felt by a member of the male warrior sodality for female sexuality. The Mórrígán also came to CúChulain at the ford. But she wished only to help him, impressed by his skill in battle. As a condition to gain her aid, she demanded that he first make love with her. This CúChulain refused to do, earning the enmity of the Mórrígán. She returned to fight with him in the shape-shifted forms of an eel, a wolf, and a hornless cow. But CúChulain defeated her each time.[17]

When CúChulain spurned the Mórrígán's sexual proposal, he again adhered to the code of the warrior sodality. He would engage in sexual relations with females only if he was ordered to do so by his leader or if he was in a position of complete dominance. But the Mórrígán was an immortal of the Tuatha Dé Danaan. She returned to humble this impudent human male. And CúChulain was willing to risk death rather than submit to female control of his sexuality.

After the war with Queen Maev came to a favourable conclusion for Ulster, CúChulain's battles did not end. On his final adventure, he was mortally wounded while facing a host of enemies. Weakened from loss of blood, he tied himself to a stone pillar, to a symbol of his phallus, and continued to fight until death overcame him. Only when Badb the Skald Crow landed on his shoulder and pecked at his flesh did his foes dare approach CúChulain's corpse. And in the end, the female force embodied in the bird aspect of the Mórrígán prevailed over the model member of the male warrior sodality.

In their sexual relationships, both CúChulain and Maev remained aloof from their partners, struggling to bend them to their will. They did not seem to recognize sexuality as a means to express love and achieve intimacy. But Maev and CúChulain did not represent the full spectrum of Celtic attitudes towards sexuality. Other myths revealed a softer viewpoint of the physical relationship between people, usually occurring when a resident of the Otherworld coupled with a mortal.

In the land of the Tuatha Dé Danaan, Étain was the second of Midir's wives. Midir displayed such desire for her that she earned the jealous hatred of Fuamnach, Midir's first wife. Fuamnach transformed Étain into a butterfly and summoned a great tempest to blow her into the realm of mortals. There she fell into a drinking cup, was swallowed by a woman, and passed into the woman's womb. Eventually, she was reborn as a mortal.[18]

In the polygamous and polyandrous relationships common to the Celts, jealousy among the multiple spouses must have been a common occurrence. The plight of Étain acted as a cautionary tale to encourage men and women to spread the devotion equally among their official sexual partners.

Reincarnation through ingestion of an insect was also a frequent motif in Celtic myth. Under certain circumstances, a woman or female animal could conceive without a sexual liaison by eating a magical insect. This did not imply that the Celts were unaware of the link between intercourse and pregnancy. But it did indicate that a mystical means existed for women to dispense with the services of men and still realize the potential of their latent fertility.

Étain grew up in the realm of mortals with no memory of her past life in the Otherworld. Eventually, she married Eochy. But Eochy's brother, Ailill, fell in love with her and he grew ill from his frustrated desire. Étain readily agreed to sleep with him to cure his malady.

Étain offered her sexuality as an act of love and compassion. There was no hint that she wished to use Ailill's desire for her in order to gain power over him or to harm her husband. This approach to sexuality contrasted sharply with Maev's and CúChulain's use of sex to achieve dominance.

What the cycles of Celtic myth did not contain also revealed a great deal about sexual attitudes. For example, no mention was made of brothels. In the Roman influenced lands to the south, men could pay money to enjoy the sexual favours of boys or women. This acted as a legitimate outlet for male sexual energy restricted by the rigid rules governing marriage and sexual relationships. The Celts, however, had no need of the prostitute. If a man or woman desired more sex than their present partner could offer, they could easily take another lover. Although the Celts exchanged sex for power, the notion of men paying women to experience sex for its own sake was alien to them.

In the Celtic myths, there was no direct evidence of homosexual encounters. The bards may have rejected the mythic quality of any sexual relationships that were infertile by their very nature. But this does not mean that homosexuality was nonexistent. Among the warrior sodalities with their contempt for female sexuality, male contacts with other men were likely to have occurred. There is some evidence that homosexuality was practised as part of some religious rituals.[19] And in the Brehon Law, male homosexuality was cited as grounds for a wife to divorce her husband.

Ritual virginity or castration was also absent from Celtic myth. There were no groups of males or females permanently dedicating their sexuality to an ideal represented by a deity. For the Celts, control of sexual urges was not a religious issue. And the indulgence displayed in their myths suggested that powers greater than human encouraged frequent sexual relations.

*

The information gleaned from Roman observations and the existing body of Celtic myth showed that the pre-Christian Celts had a sexual ethic far different from their European neighbours to the south. Sexual relationships between people were innocent in that they did not carry with them a burden of guilt and social disgrace. Men and women were not ashamed of the urges of their bodies and recognized them as natural, pleasurable and even religious.

But the Celts did not live in isolation. In Gaul and Roman Britain, foreign ideas and philosophy were forcibly imposed on them, gradually altering the way they thought about themselves and the world around them. Even in remote areas like Ireland and Scotland which remained politically independent through much of the Middle Ages, new points of view infiltrated the society from outside contact. Eventually the Celts found themselves thoroughly enmeshed in the Christian sexual ethic.

3

Christian Sexuality

In 380 AD, a Christian Celt named Pelagius left his homeland to journey to the city of Rome. The Christian philosopher Jerome described him as 'a great mountain-dog through whom the devil barks.'[1] Another adversary of his exhibited the traditional Roman disdain for the Celts by dismissing him as 'full of Irish porridge.'[2] Although his Latin contemporaries believed he was a Briton, he may have been of Irish or Scottish descent. But all accounts of Pelagius agreed that he was a large man who enjoyed a good meal.

During the time Pelagius lived in Rome, the Empire was in disarray. Barbarian tribes who had formerly guarded the borders had rebelled, encouraged by the dwindling power of the Emperor. Goths, Huns and Vandals prowled the distant provinces, casting a hungry eye at the treasures amassed for centuries in the imperial city. Outmanoeuvred and outfought on the field of battle, the once mighty legions seemed helpless to repel the intruders. Even the Emperor had abandoned Rome, moving his court to Milan. And to the citizens of the once great city, it appeared as if the end of days prophesied by the Christians were at hand.

After living in the city for many years, Pelagius grew disturbed by the frequent lapses of morality he observed among the Christian people of Rome.[3] By moral laxity, he did not mean unrestrained sexuality. With his Celtic background, he did not view sex as inherently harmful to human spirituality. And the Roman Christian church had not fully linked morality with sexuality at this time.

Instead, the immorality troubling Pelagius was an attitude

of uncaring selfishness among the Romans. Theft was wide-spread and murder for profit commonplace. Aristocrats hoarded their wealth in secret troves, unmoved by the suffering of slaves and the poor. The necessities of life grew scarce as people struggled desperately to accumulate gold and silver and jewels. Pelagius felt as if the very centre of Western Christianity had abandoned its humanity, ignoring the teachings of Christ.

When Pelagius examined the cause of the outrageous behaviour of the Romans, he discovered that the people believed their immoral acts were justified by the new doctrine of original sin. According to this idea spread by Augustine of Hippo, human nature was inherently corrupt because of the sin of Adam and Eve in Eden. People were helpless to control their vile nature and were not really responsible for their evil deeds. Their only hope was to abandon themselves to the Christian God who would provide 'grace' to bring them to salvation. But meanwhile, they might as well be wicked since all would be forgiven in the end.

This idea of original sin which absolved individual responsibility for evil acts was strange and foreign to Pelagius. In his Celtic homeland to the north, people assumed that they could exercise some control over their destiny, that they could choose between good and evil. He believed that perfection was possible for humanity and the attempt to achieve it was a solemn obligation. Any talk of original sin was merely an excuse for the moral depravity of the Romans during the time of the collapse of Empire. But the Celtic concepts of Pelagius placed him in direct opposition to Augustine of Hippo. And in the ensuing clash of ideas, Pelagius found himself denounced a heretic. But he was not the only victim of Augustine's theories. Augustine also permanently destroyed the innocence of Western sexuality.

Augustine of Hippo managed to fuse hatred of sexuality and pleasure into a philosophy adopted by the Roman Christians. More than any other Christian writer, he was responsible for the severing of love from sexuality in the West. But he was not a particularly innovative thinker. He merely borrowed ideas from the past and transformed them into a context acceptable to Christians.

Hostility towards sex appeared in the medical writings of the Greeks. Pythagoras believed that all sexual relations were harmful, leading to a general weakening of the body. Plato praised an Olympic athlete for wisely avoiding sex during training. The Greek belief in the benefit of sexual abstention influenced the Roman physician Galen and the Christian medical practitioners who followed him.[4]

The Stoics of Rome also found sexuality philosophically suspect. They saw sexual relations only in terms of pleasure and rejected them as spiritually harmful. Seneca claimed that it was foolish for a person to immoderately love their spouse. True love came only from reason, not from passion. And since desire was involuntary, the mind could be clouded by the sexual passion felt for a spouse. He went as far as to admonish men for making love with their pregnant wives, creating the concept of fornication within marriage.[5]

Abstention from sexual relations was mandatory for the clergy of several pagan cults. In Rome, the virgins dedicated to Vesta would face death at the hands of their sisters if they slept with a man. The Phrygian priests of Cybele viewed themselves as lovers of the goddess and willingly castrated themselves to avoid the risk of betraying the goddess with a mortal woman.

By the time Augustine was born in 354 AD, the pagan movement to sever love from sexuality was already several centuries old. Not to be outdone by their religious rivals, the Christians slowly adopted a code of celibacy for their own priesthood. Convened in Spain during the early part of the fourth century AD, the Synod of Elvira declared that married priests and bishops had to forgo sexual relations with their wives from that time onwards. The rule of Elvira applied only to Spain, but was proposed for church-wide adoption at the Council of Nicea in 325 AD. It was accepted in modified form as a prohibition against marriage by bachelors who entered the priesthood.[6]

The need for clerical celibacy may have also had roots in the increasing level of hierarchical stratification among the Roman Christians. If priests and bishops could freely produce children, there was a real risk that a priestly class would develop, passing church offices from parent to child. Such a practice would exclude from the clergy those without sufficient wealth or family connections to gain admission.

As Augustine grew to maturity, he must have been aware of the Christian controversies focusing on the sexuality of priests. But in his early days, Augustine wanted little to do with this religion that had come to dominate the Roman Empire. He followed the teachings of Mani, a Persian whose ideas had considerable influence throughout the Middle East. Mani felt that salvation lay only in releasing the goodness or light that demons had imprisoned in matter. The earth and all the pleasures found in it were evil creations of darkness, designed to trap goodness. Sex was a hindrance to salvation since reproduction merely created another poor soul caged in a demon-made body.[7] And women were seducers to prevent the salvation of the Elect, the perfect male followers of Mani.

The Elect were celibate men predestined to achieve salvation. Below them in importance were the Hearers. These were men who were barred from salvation because they could not renounce the material world completely and abstain from sex. Women were dehumanized, regarded as sexual evil incarnate.[8]

Many of Mani's concepts were themselves echoes of earlier ideas focusing on the religious supremacy of the sun. Centuries before, the Persian Zoroaster spoke of the battle between light and dark. Hebrew and Mesopotamian cosmology associated angels with light. The suffix 'el' in names such as Rapha-el, Micha-el and Gabri-el indicated brightness.[9]

As a scholar, Augustine was probably aware of the parallel Middle Eastern traditions supporting Manicheanism. But Augustine was not an ardent disciple of Mani. He lived for fifteen years with a woman he never named in his writings. Out of wedlock, she bore him a son. Augustine claimed that he refused to marry this woman because she was from a different social class. But perhaps Augustine chose not to marry because this would place him firmly in the less prestigious Manichean class of Hearers.

In 384 AD, Augustine was appointed professor of rhetoric at the Emperor's court in Milan. At the urging of his Christian mother, he sent his mistress away. And this unnamed woman vowed never to love another. But Augustine scorned her devotion and immediately found another bed mate while his mother was arranging a socially suitable marriage.

Eventually, Augustine grew disillusioned by the oversimplifications of Manicheanism and in 387 AD decided to become a Christian. He accepted baptism from Ambrose of Milan, a man whose own writings betrayed a bias against sexuality.[10] Immediately, Augustine decided to embrace a life of ascetic celibacy. He cast aside his new lover and abandoned his plans for marriage. To justify such heartless treatment of his female companions, he developed a contempt for sexuality. In his mind, he severed love for another from love for an ideal. And he fostered the notion of original sin to absolve any guilt he felt for his callous behaviour, claiming that he was helpless to overcome his base nature before he had received the gift of 'grace' from the Christian God.

Returning to Africa, he started a monastic community and surrounded himself with men who were sworn to celibacy. Eventually, his prolific writings, his skill at delivering sermons, and his connections at the Imperial Court, encouraged the people of Hippo to ask him to become their bishop. And after he was installed in office, he refined his doctrines, fusing Manichean loathing of sexuality with Christianity.

Augustine began with the Manichean proposition that people, as long as they are mortal, must also be wretched and sinful. He Christianized the idea by claiming that this sorry condition was the result of the sin of Adam and Eve which placed an enduring burden on humanity. The transmission of this original sin from generation to generation occurred during the despised act of sex. And only 'grace' from a benevolent god could keep a person from wallowing in evil.[11]

Marriage provided the only permissible outlet for human sexual energy. But the objective in marriage was reproduction,

Celtic Sexuality

not pleasure. Augustine encouraged people to engage in sex as a reproductive duty while somehow ignoring the pleasure created by the act.

Augustine also expanded the Christian concept of predestination first suggested by Paul of Tarsus. Again borrowing from Mani, he claimed that the Christian God knew beforehand who would achieve salvation and who would be damned. Infants who died prior to Christian baptism were doomed to hell by original sin, despite their personal innocence. This encouraged people to embrace evil, since good or evil deeds did not alter the irrevocable fate of the saved and the damned. However, Augustine's ideas of predestination were eventually rejected by the Christian community.

During the time of Augustine, theology was regarded as a form of science. Thinkers proposed a theorem which in turn generated new ideas and new questions. The fact that theological theorems were not capable of proof did not trouble the people who produced them. It merely took an edict of the Bishop of Rome or an agreement by a church council to transform an unprovable idea into an indisputable fact.

As Bishop of Hippo, Augustine used his position and the connections he had established at the Imperial Court to further the acceptance of his ideas. Since Christianity was the official state religion, if the Emperor accepted a particular doctrine, it became the law of the land backed by civil authority. Because the Bishop of Rome was not yet universally accepted as the supreme leader of Christians, they exerted only limited influence on the Emperors.[12] Augustine successfully managed to convince both Emperor Honorius and Pope Innocent I that his view of the transmission of original sin through sex was true and correct.

With official sanction from Rome, Augustine used letters and two full length works, the *City of God* and *Confessions,* to spread his vision of sexually sterile Christianity to all parts of the Roman Empire. And as the Empire entered its death throes, amid the anarchy created by the collapse of central government, Augustine's thoughts survived to become a fundamental precept of Western Christianity.

The more Pelagius examined the views of Augustine, the more disturbed he became. He was certain that sin was a voluntary imitation of Adam's act in Eden, not an inherent human condition. Any 'grace' that the Christian God might offer came in the form of forgiveness of sin. And he could not understand the basis of Augustine's link between sexuality and sin.[13]

So Pelagius took his pen in hand to refute Augustine's ideas. In a simple and straightforward manner, he pointed out how Augustine's labyrinth of logic wandered down twisted paths. But this was a grave mistake for this displaced Celt living so far from his homeland. He had no access to the Bishop of Rome or the Imperial Court in Milan. He was merely one more clergyman in a city overflowing with priests and monks.

Attacked for his opposition to Augustine, Pelagius thought it would be prudent if he left Rome. This was a fortunate decision, since a short time later in the year 412 AD, Alaric and his Visigoths sacked the city. But in his choice of destinations, Pelagius was not so wise. He went to Africa, near to Hippo where Augustine held absolute ecclesiastical power. He was accompanied by his friend, the lawyer Celestius.

When Augustine learned that his doctrinal enemy now resided close to his theocratic citadel, he immediately wrote several letters denouncing Pelagius. Rather than defend his own logic, Augustine twisted the words of Pelagius, portraying him as a monster stabbing at the heart of Christianity. And Pelagius again fled, leaving Celestius behind to refute the charges against him.

In 412 AD, Augustine convened the Council of Carthage to condemn Pelagius. Since Augustine's ideas were officially sanctioned by the Emperor and the Pope, he did not have to defend his own position. It was enough that Pelagius opposed Augustine. The unfortunate Celestius was branded a heretic by this council, but he managed to flee to Ephesus.

Eventually, Pelagius arrived in Jerusalem where he cleared himself at a specially convened council in that city. Enraged when he heard the news, Augustine wrote a letter to Innocent I at the new papal palace in Ravenna. The Bishop of Rome had moved his court to escape the anarchy following Alaric's plundering. And in that letter, Augustine persuaded Innocent to excommunicate Pelagius.

This should have been the end of Augustine's troubles with Pelagius. But when Zossima succeeded Innocent I as Bishop of Rome in 417 AD, Pelagius' friend Celestius appeared in Ravenna and obtained an audience with the new Pope. At Celestius' urging, Zossima read Pelagius' work *On Faith* and agreed that it contained nothing heretical. He lifted the ban of excommunication on Pelagius.

Augustine was outraged. He convened yet another council which refused to ratify Zossima's decision. Augustine also called on his friends in the Imperial Court to influence the Emperor Honorius to issue a decree denouncing Pelagius. Faced with rebellion within the church and a rift with the still powerful civil authorities, Zossima had no choice but to revoke his decision. Pelagius was again branded a Christian heretic and remained so to this day. In 494 AD, his works were placed on the Index of Proscribed Books and any Christian who read his words risked excommunication.

Pelagius vanished after 417 AD. Some accounts claimed that he retired to a monastery in Phrygia. But perhaps he merely returned home to Britain or Ireland, weary of the insanity that seemed to grip the Christians living on the shores of the Mediterranean.

*

As a result of his successful political intrigue, Augustine stood alone as the primary Christian thinker after the fall of Rome. His pessimistic notions about the world and humanity gradually permeated the Roman Christian church. And as this particular sect of Christians slowly gained spiritual and temporal power, the anti-sexual values of Augustine spread through Western society.

Based on Augustine's thought, the process of dehumanizing women accelerated. Women were officially categorized by the Roman church as 'evil stimulants' instead of partners to men.

Clergymen were exhorted to avoid the company of all women, including their sisters and mothers on the theory that the mere presence of a female was sufficient to generate involuntary lust in a man.[14] The only acceptable woman was one sworn to virginity. And even she was suspect.

Acceptance of the ideal of virginity and belief that all sex transmitted original sin could not instantly strip the sworn male celibate of his sexuality. He had to be ever vigilant against the snares of women, against the temptations of the weaker gender who were incapable of controlling their own base desires. All parts of the female body were considered erotic dangers. Hair had to be covered, hands hidden, and dresses had to reach to the ground. There was even serious consideration of forcing women to veil their faces.[15]

If Roman Christian society had been unwilling to accept restrictions against sex and women, they would not have become widespread. Augustine would have remained a pathological aberration instead of rising to prominence. But for centuries, the relations between men and women in Mediterranean lands had been growing more distant, leaving both genders with a sense of inadequacy.

Both Rome and the Eastern Mediterranean countries it conquered were strict patriarchies. A woman's behaviour and sexuality were closely guarded by her husband or father. And for both parties in a marriage, the relationship often seemed detached and remote, lacking intimacy. Men frequently sought love in the arms of concubines or prostitutes who held low social status. Married women suffered sexual and emotional deprivation. Female prostitutes, concubines and slaves could form no relationship with their male partners beyond the sexual.[16] So when Augustine claimed that love for an ideal was superior to sexual love, many people were willing to try this alternative. He merely supported a popular viewpoint of his day with pseudo-Christian theory, reflecting a paradigm of the culture instead of inventing it.

Initially, the ideas of Augustine had little impact on the distant lands of Ireland and Britain. The Christian Celts were quite happy with their sexual relationships and were not

searching for an alternative. They had integrated their culture
with the teachings of Christ, creating their own form of Christianity that did not depend on Mediterranean guidance. It took
several centuries for the Roman Church to sufficiently expand
its power to come into direct conflict with the Celtic Church.
And like Pelagius, the Celts did not have adequate strength to
successfully resist the attack.

4

Pagans and Christians

Christianity spread through Western Europe in many different ways. Sometimes, the religion was forced upon a vanquished nation by the blade of a conqueror's sword. Other times, the promise of great power whispered in a monarch's ears brought conversion by royal decree. And whenever individuals grew disillusioned with their existing beliefs, the new faith offered solace. Fear, force and mystery were the customary tools employed by the Christians to achieve religious primacy. But in the Celtic islands of Britain and Ireland, the religion initially expanded on its own merit without physical or emotional coercion.

In Britain, Christianity arrived with the Roman soldiers who occupied the southern part of the island. Some of the invaders were Christians, secretly clinging to their beliefs even during the periods when the Emperors outlawed the new faith. And with typical Christian enthusiasm, they preached to the native Celts, converting the clans in the Roman-occupied areas.

By the fourth century AD, the Christian faith was widespread in the urban centres established by the Romans. The Latin word *paganus* meant 'rustic'. Eventually the word evolved in meaning to describe people who clung to pre-Christian religions, indicating that Christianity was concentrated in cities and large towns. Archeological excavations in Britain agree with this premise, uncovering crosses an other symbols of the Christian religion only in urban locations. The earliest inscriptions on walls and pottery date from approximately 315

AD, the time when Emperor Constantine sanctioned the open practice of Christianity.[1]

After the Emperors abandoned the costly defence of distant Britain, Christianity continued to grow and prosper without direct guidance from Rome. The Celts created a local version of Christian worship unique to the society it served. But the Celtic divergence from Mediterranean Christian practices and doctrines was not due to isolation alone. Throughout the fifth and sixth centuries AD, prominent Celtic clergy travelled to Rome, including such monastic founders as Ninian, Finian, and Enda. By attending European councils and synods, the Celts remained aware of the evolution of Christian doctrine and of the internal administrative organization promoted by the Bishop of Rome. Yet they did not believe that any foreign authority was entitled to legitimate supremacy over their faith. They rejected the Roman system of dioceses led by bishops with the power to control all local religious matters.[2] Celtic priests owed allegiance only to the scriptures and to their clan. Abbots and abbesses held more prestige than bishops, directing the development of Celtic religious doctrine and practices.[3] Eventually, the beliefs and customs of the Celtic Christians deviated greatly from the dogma sanctioned by the Bishop of Rome.

But not all Celts exclusively followed their own brand of Christianity. After the new religion became established, a significant minority of clergymen came to believe the doctrines of the Bishop of Rome were superior to their local version. In Britain, the Roman school of clergy called the 'Romani' were encouraged by the successful conversion of the invading Saxons by missionaries sent by Pope Gregory I. The gradual growth of Saxon political supremacy supported the Romani movement among the Celtic Christians.

But the majority of the early Christians in Britain and Ireland were merely druids in a new guise. Steeped in centuries-old tradition, the druid priests of the Celts did not look upon the new religion as a competing faith, as a threat to their power and their time-honoured beliefs. Instead, the druids saw Christ as complementing their existing values. They embraced the new creed and merged many of their pagan viewpoints and practices into Christianity. Writing in the sixth century AD, the bard Taliesin was reputed to claim that 'Christ in Asia was a new thing; but there never was a time when the Druids of Britain held not his doctrine'.[4]

In the Celtic tongue, the druids were known as the *áes-dana*, as men and women who were especially gifted.[5] Their function in Celtic society was complex. They spoke the law, interpreting past custom for the needs of the moment. They acted as shamans, as guides for the spiritual journey exploring the mysteries of the self and the world. In the role of bard, they sang the songs of the past, recalling the glory and wisdom of days long gone. And as satirists, they heaped ridicule on foolish kings and queens. Just below royalty in privilege and status, the *áes-dana* were the sages of Celtic society, the people who could explain the meaning of events and dictate the appropriate response.

In general, the druids viewed nature and the material world as a single spiritual entity. Their supreme being was inseparable from the universe itself. Sprawling oaks, billowing clouds, and frothing seas were all manifestations of spirituality. And people were part of the world, connected directly to the spirituality of the universe. Other forms of life were also holy and possessed a part of the essence of the god-head. The goal of the druid was an inner illumination, the achievement of a sacred awareness of the human link with the universe.[6]

Because early Celtic Christianity developed as an offshoot of druidism, it was not initially influenced by the Near Eastern and Roman perceptions that the world was the creation of a male god who resided in a separate place from the world he created. Because the Christian supreme being was detached from creation, it was not difficult to imagine that the earth was a realm of evil, populated and controlled by demon spirits who opposed the plans of the good god. The Celtic world view could not easily accommodate such a pessimistic analysis of the universe.

Both before and after the arrival of Christianity, druids would summon the elemental forces of nature to create a protective spell of magic. They called this spell a *lorica*, a breastplate of spiritual power. By chanting the invocation, they enlisted the aid of the universe itself to shield them from harm. The *lorica* attributed to Saint Patrick could have been spoken by any druid before the arrival of Christianity.

> I arise today
> Through the strength of heaven
> Light of sun
> Radiance of moon
> Splendour of fire
> Speed of lightning
> Swiftness of wind
> Depth of sea
> Stability of earth
> Firmness of rock.[7]

Patrick did not invoke a god external to the universe to create this protective spell. Instead he called upon the powers of earth, sky, and sea.

The druids also related to Christ as an epic hero similar to CúChulain or Finn. Their mythology celebrated the battle of the individual against any type of outside domination whether material or spiritual. It appeared to the Celts that the Gospels of Christ echoed this traditional mythic theme. Christ came from the Otherworld to show mortals how to find the way to the mystical land of life after death. He acted like a druid, controlling the elements, performing miracles and dispensing wisdom. He was beset by enemies who persecuted him until he died. And his final triumph of resurrection fitted neatly into the Celtic vision of the heroic.

Other Christian ideas seemed familiar to the druids. Baptism was a symbolic reincarnation using water, an elemental force. Just as the druid initiate was reborn into a higher state of knowledge, so too did baptism grant deeper insight.

When Christ entered human form, he engaged in metempsychosis, in spiritual shape-shifting. This ritual was accepted custom among the druid shaman who assumed the spirit form of the wolf or the salmon in a quest for greater wisdom.[8] It also echoed in part the adventures of Étain who left the Otherworld to enjoy a rebirth in a new body among mortals.

The Old Testament of the Bible could also compete effectively with Celtic mythology and saga poetry. It related the epic adventures of a warlike people, complete with stories of kings and fools, of wicked men and heroic women. It spoke of law and morality and had more than a few tales stimulating prurient interest. And in the New Testament, the decapitation of John the Baptist seemed to reflect Celtic head lore, the belief that the skull was the seat of the soul's power.

The Celts also understood Christianity's rejection of material wealth. Personal property among the Celts was limited to household goods, clothing, jewellery and weapons. All necessities of life such as cattle, land, and crops were held in common by the clan. The *poltach* custom required that surplus goods be distributed among the needy to ease their suffering. These almost socialist attitudes towards property dovetailed nicely with the theoretical tenets of Christianity.

Because of the similarities between the druids and the Christians, there was little hostility to the new religion. But the Celts did not regard religious and philosophic concepts as matters serious enough to fight over. Christian monarchs did not require their subjects to submit to the new faith. And pagan rulers were indifferent to the Christian practices of their people unless they interfered with efficient government. If a few overly zealous monks wanted to shut themselves up in bleak monasteries, it was a matter of little importance to anyone not directly involved. Absent from Celtic Britain and Ireland was the fanatic zeal of both pagans and Christians which elsewhere created a lengthy list of martyrs on both sides of the issue of religious conversion. In Ireland, no one was ritually murdered as a deterrent to the practice of a religion until well after the arrival of the English in the twelfth century AD.

*

In the numerologically significant year 432 AD, great events

happened for the Christians. The Council of Ephesus proclaimed Mary to be the Mother of God, enhancing the power of
the cult of Mary. And the Irish annals declared this to be the
year that Patrick arrived in Ireland. But many historians now
agree that the more likely date for the beginning of Patrick's
mission was 461 AD.[9]

When Patrick came to Ireland, the southern part of the
island already had long-established Christian communities.
For centuries, there had been considerable commerce between
Wales and Ireland, exchanging ideas as well as trade goods.
Christianity probably came to Ireland with merchants, sailors
and adventurers who spoke to their Celtic cousins about the
new faith. To describe the unusual religious concepts, Latin
loan words migrated from Britain and appeared in Irish during
the fourth century AD. Prior to Patrick, a Gaulish bishop
named Palladius and three companions had been sent to tend
to the needs of the Irish Christians.

Patrick was no stranger to Ireland. He was a Briton from an
upper class Christian family who had been captured as a
hostage during a raid by the Irish king, Milchu. For many
years, Patrick was a herdsman in Ireland until he managed to
escape. In Gaul, he studied for the priesthood and resolved to
return to Ireland as a missionary. He wrote of his early experiences in his book, the *Confessio*. But he left gaps and incon-
sistencies in his narrative giving rise to many legends
concerning his life and his deeds. The source for many of the
fantastic occurrences attributed to Patrick was the *Life of
Padraig* written by Miurchú in the seventh century AD. In this
work, Patrick acted like a druid, performing miracles, raising
the dead, and commanding the elements. Miurchú's portrayal
of Patrick probably echoed the expectations for the behaviour
of a bishop in his own time.[10]

Although he was a British Celt, Patrick did not seem to have
a firm grasp of Irish Celtic customs. He wore plain clothing
when he first went to speak with Laeghire, the High King of
Ireland. Since the Irish recognized only personal property, the
quality of a person's adornment was a measure of status. King
Laeghire and his court mocked Patrick when they saw his

simple garments. To remedy this oversight, Patrick hired mercenaries to create an ostentatious display and made gifts of gold and silver to prominent people. Presumably the funds for such extravagances were provided by the Roman Christians of Gaul.

No doubt King Laeghire had heard of the Christian religion before Patrick's arrival. But he was not greatly impressed by the apparent vagabond who came to call on him. He did not express much interest in Patrick's ideas. But in keeping with the Irish tradition of religious tolerance, he gave permission for Patrick to preach wherever he chose.

Patrick decided to go north and west to the citadel of Emain Mhacha, to the seat of power of the Clan Uliad. In this part of Ireland, Christianity was largely unknown and the people must have viewed Patrick as an amusing novelty. Legend had him founding Armagh as the site of his church located a few miles from the main fortress. Some four hundred years later, the Bishop of Armagh claimed ecclesiastical primacy over all Ireland based on a chain of authority stretching back to Patrick.

But Patrick was not as successful in drawing the Irish to Christianity as tradition suggests. He tried to institute a Roman style hierarchy to administer the church, a system the Celts found excessively rigid. Most of the work of conversion was actually performed much later by wandering monks in the sixth century AD. Large pockets of pagan practice survived until the time of the English invasion of Ireland eight centuries after the death of Patrick. In the twelfth century AD, the Norman chronicler Geraldus Cambrensis recorded a ceremony for the installation of an Ulster clan chieftain which was thoroughly pagan. Before the prospective leader could assume power, he first had to engage in public intercourse with a mare. Then the unlucky horse was killed and a broth made of her flesh to be distributed among the onlookers.[11]

Throughout the Middle Ages, Ireland was a land ruled by countless petty kings and queens. Each clan chief styled himself a monarch, owing allegiance only to his people. Nominally, there was an elected High King, but his authority was not universally recognized throughout the entire island. This led to frequent conflict as High Kings tried to impose their will on reluctant subjects. And while Patrick was blithely preaching at Armagh, the politics of the time engulfed him. The High King Laeghire and his Clan Uí Néill quarrelled with Clan Uliad, driving them from their stronghold at Emain Mhacha. The Uliad emigrated eastward and Patrick accompanied his flock. He died in Downpatrick close to the Irish Sea.

As a Christian Celt, Patrick did not appear greatly concerned with the sexual practices of the Irish people. Later tradition has Patrick condemning the Celtic marital customs as adulterous. But his letter to the British chieftain Corocticus did contain some direct evidence of Patrick's attitude toward sexuality. It admonished Corocticus for 'distributing baptized damsels as rewards, and for the sake of miserable temporal things which verily pass away in a moment like a cloud of smoke which is dispersed by the wind.'[12] Presumably, if the kidnapped women were not Christian, Patrick would approve of Corocticus' behaviour. But this statement did betray the Roman Christian belief that pleasure was transitory, an impediment to salvation.

*

The early Celtic Christians did not initially tamper with the existing sexual habits of their people. Since persuasion was the only means for the new religion to gain acceptance, its beliefs could not appear too alien to the ways of the Celts. The Christians could neither muster armies to impose their will nor offer vast wealth or power to monarchs. So any of the clergy who knew of Augustine's sterile vision of sexuality rejected it as a Roman doctrine with no application to Britain and Ireland.

Generally, the Celts seemed to have little difficulty accepting the paradox lying at the core of the imported Christian philosophy. Virgins gave birth, death brought eternal life, and enemies were loved instead of hated. The contradictions were unquestionable, buttressed by faith, by a willing belief in the unbelievable. And as Christianity spread, people came to regard the fusion of dissimilar concepts as perfectly natural.

St. Scuithín was famous for loving his virginity and for loving women as well. This paradox was necessary to make Scuithín acceptable to both Celts and Christians.[13] For the Celts, sexuality was as basic as eating. In order for the new religion to succeed, some compromise with existing sexual customs had to be achieved. Scuithín could not be considered manly and a person to emulate unless he loved women. So the Christians merged libidinous behaviour with their concept of chastity. Eventually the paradox of Scuithín became so commonplace that few noticed the inherent lack of logic in the linking of opposing ideas.

The many Lives of the Saints written to chronicle the adventures of prominent Christians revealed the persistence of pre-Christian sexual attitudes. For example, male bishops and abbots practised the custom of cupping their genitals with their hand to affirm an oath. They swore by the sacred seed within them that their words were true and correct.

Like the mythic heroes and heroines before them, Celtic saints were often born from unusual sexual circumstances. Creda was the mother of St. Báithín, the second abbot of Iona. She was a good and holy woman who frequently washed her hands and face in a small pool outside a church. One day, a thief hid in a tree over her head. Overcome by her fair face and shapely form, he secretly masturbated, allowing his semen to fall onto a bed of watercress. Perhaps intentionally, perhaps accidentally, Creda ate the watercress and miraculously gave birth to Báithín.[14] This allowed Creda to remain technically virginal while granting Christian sanction to the Celtic belief in orally induced reproduction under wondrous circumstances.

By magic, a mysterious stranger deceived St. Lonan's mother by assuming the form of her lover, much as Uther Pendragon duped King Arthur's mother, Igraine. St. Cuimine Foda and St. Cennyd were born from incestuous liaisons, similar to CúChulain. St. Beuno's elderly parents had not indulged in sex for twelve years when his mother amazingly found herself pregnant.[15]

The unique sexual unions producing the Christian saints were not an exclusive invention of the Celts. In virtually every culture from Aztec to Mongol, dramatic mystery shrouds the conception of the gods, demigods, and heroes of myth. But unlike the Christians of continental Europe, the Celts preserved the explicit nature of the sexual encounter experienced by the saint's parents. They did not strip human passion from the act of conception to eliminate the human emotions and responses of the saint's mother.

Since the Celtic Christians did not initially adhere to the Mediterranean paradox that females had souls but were inherently evil, women retained the high status they enjoyed during exclusively pagan times. The matrilinear society of the Celts traced ancestry through the mother, since the exact identity of a father could never be proven. The surnames of prominent men often included the name of their mother as in Conchobhar mac Nessa, Conchobhar the son of Nessa. Any reduction in the status of women would reduce the pride that people felt in their personal heritage.

In Ireland and Britain, the Christians initially made no rule against marriage for the clergy. Even ascetic hermits were allowed spouses. If the regulations of a particular abbot or abbess forbade marriage, the monks and nuns were free to join a more liberal community. Unlike their Roman contemporaries, Celtic priests enjoyed unrestricted sexual relations with their spouses. News of the various edicts of church councils regarding the chastity of the clergy was slow to reach the remote Celtic lands. And when the Celts did learn of the Roman Christian rules cramping clerical sexuality, they viewed them as the local practices of foreigners having no universal validity.

Many of the Christian monasteries established in Ireland and Britain were 'mixed houses' where male and female ascetics lived, worked and prayed under the same roof. Due to the religious equality of men and women, there was no distinction between monastery and convent. The Abbess Hilda presided over the largest of these integrated monasteries at Hartlepool in Celtic Britain. The possibility that sexual relationships would develop between the men and women in the mixed houses was not initially viewed as a deterrent to their operation. Only after the Roman Christians gained influence in Celtic lands were the mixed houses considered scandalous.

In keeping with the druid tradition, women acted as clergy in the Celtic church. Serving as conhospitalers, women commonly distributed communion during the Christian ritual, providing a link between the priest and the people. Occasionally, women were ordained as priests and Beverly, the disciple of Hilda, rose to the level of bishop.

In addition to their continued acceptance of human sexuality, the Celts developed other unique practices which diverged from other Christian sects. The clergy wore the tonsure of St. John, requiring avowed religious to shave the hair on the entire front half of the skull. This hair pattern had previously been worn by druids to indicate their status. However, the Roman Christians found this tonsure blasphemous, associating it with Simon Magus who was Peter's arch-rival in the early days of the religion. The Roman clergy insisted on a small circular tonsure on the back of the head.[16] Opinions varied as to the meaning of this hair pattern. The Venerable Bede claimed the shaved circle commemorated Christ's crown of thorns.[17] Other historians of the period believed it originated from the tonsure of the Roman slave.

In Celtic lands, bishops did not exercise the same influence their colleagues enjoyed in other parts of the former Roman Empire. Due to the decentralized political structure of their society, the Celts resisted Christian efforts to set up a rigid ecclesiastical hierarchy which focused power in the hands of a few prominent people. The absence of large cities to serve as administrative centres for bishops also hampered the establishment of a diocesan system along Roman lines.

The Celts celebrated Easter on a different date from the Roman church. They calculated the date based on the day of the week fourteen days after the first full moon after the vernal equinox. Although this was the traditional reckoning for the first five hundred years after Christ, it occasionally caused Easter and Passover to occur on the same date.[18] The Roman

Christians felt that this was improper and altered the calculation in 525 AD. Although the retrospect of many centuries may make this seem like an insignificant variation, the Celtic and Roman Christians eventually quarrelled bitterly over the correct computation of the date of Easter.

The Celts brought a large measure of their own heritage to their practice of Christianity. Incorporating their existing rituals and viewpoints into the new religion, they created a faith reflecting their culture. But the new ideas also introduced change into Celtic society, sometimes subtle, sometimes dramatic. And the arrival of Christianity brought a wave of new perceptions that would irretrievably alter the way the Celts viewed themselves and the world they lived in.

5

Mother, Lover and Hag

When St. Brendan the Navigator was a young man, he once passed a few hours waiting in a carriage for his mentor, Bishop Erc of Kerry. An attractive girl wandered by and smiled at him.[1] Brendan was suddenly faced with many possible choices to govern his response.

He could have viewed the girl as a mother, nurturing and protective. Or he could have perceived her as a lover, warm and sensuous. He could also have seen her as a hag, as a feminine creature whose beautiful exterior concealed a destructive force unleashed as a prelude to rebirth. The paradigms of Celtic culture recognized the triple aspect of mother, lover and hag as latent roles common to all women.[2] Brendan's heritage urged him to classify the girl in accordance with one of these model viewpoints developed by the Celts to explain the meaning behind the smile of a woman. But instead of a Celtic paradigm, Brendan chose a Christian explanation for the girl's smile. He launched a physical attack, viewing her as a demon incarnate sent to rob him of his chastity.

Confronted by the girl, given no clue as to who or what she was, Brendan selected a paradigm to give meaning to her smile. Then the paradigm operated to control the interpretation he placed on the encounter. The paradigms available to Brendan were the accepted models or thought patterns which the Celts relied on to make sense of events. They moulded assumptions about the types of entities existing in the world and governed a person's reaction to normal occurrences.[3]

*

Prior to the arrival of Christianity, the Celts had developed unique cultural paradigms to explain love, death, sexuality, and all other aspects of spiritual and material experience. Embedded in myth, folklore, and behavioural anecdotes, these viewpoints were passed from one generation to another during childhood education. They acted as mental guideposts, explaining such diverse things as when to weep and when to laugh, who to love and who to hate, and how to live and how to die. They defined and limited the activities of the society, the community and the individual. Taken as a whole, they constituted the core beliefs the Celts carried with them, the notions of reality colouring the way people interacted with the world. And long before Brendan was born, a consensus within Celtic culture agreed on common paradigms to govern a man's possible response to a smiling woman.

While Celtic society at large had its mainstream paradigms, individuals like Brendan and specialized communities like the Christians developed personal paradigms. Sometimes the paradigms of an individual or community varied only slightly from the viewpoints held by the majority of people. But other times, subculture paradigms diverged greatly, resulting in conflict with the main culture.[4]

From birth, Brendan must have been thoroughly indoctrinated with the traditional paradigms of the Celts. But at some point in his life, he chose to adopt the new paradigms introduced by the Christian subculture. Once he made this decision, the Christian models for thought and behaviour validated themselves by transforming experience into something comprehensible. The girl smiled at him, perhaps from lust, perhaps from friendliness. Brendan may have felt sexually aroused. The venerated Christian Augustine portrayed women as evil harlots who tempt men. The Christian paradigm helped Brendan make sense of his awakening sexual response. Therefore Augustine's viewpoint must be correct. And if this type of thought process occurred often enough with large numbers of people, the new paradigm would become generally accepted, replacing the old model viewpoints of the mainstream culture.[5]

As Christianity became more significant in Celtic life during the fifth and sixth centuries AD, the paradigms of the Christian subculture slowly replaced the long-established viewpoints of the Celts. Initially, the Celtic Christians retained some of the paradigms of their ancestors, creating a blend of new and old beliefs. It was a time of consolidation for Christianity, a time when revolutionary religious concepts had to compete with an ancient way of life. But as Christianity became firmly rooted in Celtic society, paradigms originating in Rome and the middle East crept into Celtic thought. The acceptance of the Roman version of Christianity by the Saxons gave the foreign paradigms a firm foothold in Britain which gradually expanded until it encompassed all the Celtic lands. Eventually, pagans and Christians would view the same event and draw sharply different conclusions. Beyond the gender of Brendan's girl, a pagan Celt was capable of seeing her as a warrior, a scholar, or a leader. For those Christians who adopted Augustine's sexual pessimism, these options were not available. They could only view a woman as a potential sexual temptress.

The gradual shift toward Roman Christian paradigms occurred because the traditional Celtic paradigms failed to serve the needs of the society. Like all cultures, the model viewpoints of the Celts were not static. When crises and turmoil created radically different conditions for Celtic society, the existing paradigms had to make sense of the new and surprising occurrences. If they could not, if the traditional paradigms failed, confusion resulted.[6] In such times, the Christians were always near at hand, offering unique explanations for events based on their own view of the universe.

It was possible for the traditional paradigms of the Celts to overlook isolated events which could not be explained by existing viewpoints. But in the fifth and sixth centuries AD, the number and frequency of unusual incidents grew too large to ignore. The relentless Saxons invaded the southern part of Britain. Defeated in battle after battle, inexorably driven westward towards Cornwall and Wales, the Celts of Britain could reach no accommodation with these militant intruders. The Celts were not accustomed to the Saxon concept of total warfare which jeopardized children, the elderly and the infirm.[7]

Refugees poured into Scotland and Ireland, spreading tales of bitter conflict and unending bloodshed. The news from distant Gaul and Italy was equally bleak. Huns, Franks, and Lombards had overrun the once mighty Roman Empire, oppressing the conquered peoples in continental Europe. Even the Irish and Picts who were remote from the conflicts must have felt threatened, searching the sea coast for the ships that would bring invasion, war and hardship.

Because their society was unable to cope with the military threat posed by the Saxons, the traditional paradigms of the Celts in Britain no longer seemed valid, no longer seemed to function smoothly. People began to search for alternative viewpoints to help them make sense of the traumatic events taking place around them. In increasing numbers they turned to the Christians, to the priests and hermits who claimed to have new perceptions that would explain all things. And when the Celtic Christians themselves could formulate no answer for the questions of their followers, they turned to Rome for additional guidance.

Since Celtic Christianity was a fusion of Christian and druid beliefs, it was initially buttressed by the general paradigms of Celtic culture. As long as the traditional model concepts satisfactorily interpreted human experience, no degree of exposure to the religious doctrines of the Mediterranean could convince the Christians of Britain and Ireland to totally abandon the paradigms of their ancestors. But when the traditional Celtic explanations for events faltered, the Roman Christians were ready and able to offer alternative paradigms to fill the gap.

During the centuries when Celtic viewpoints gradually shifted toward the Roman Christian world view, some people continued clinging to the ancient ways of interpreting events. In isolated glens and valleys, the old and familiar paradigms were safe and comfortable, still able to function as viable models for thought and behaviour. The result was a lengthy spiritual conflict as new ideas battled with old for dominance over the Celtic soul. Eventually the Roman Christian paradigms attracted a sufficient number of followers to achieve a critical mass of acceptance and became the norm for the Celts.

The traditional paradigms were considered quaint and old fashioned, a carryover from a barbarous age. They survived only in the fringes of Celtic society, an echo from a forgotten past.

And as a result of the changing paradigms of the Celts, Brendan the Navigator rewarded the smile of a hapless girl with a beating. While this particular incident may never have happened, the Christians recorded it as a parable to demonstrate how vigorously a man should guard his chastity. By enshrining the story in the *Life of Brendan* written centuries after his death, it became a part of the myth, lore, and anecdotes which transmitted the Roman Christian paradigms from one generation to another. And the triumph of Augustine's passionless intercourse over the bold sexuality of Maev, CúChulain and Angus óg was complete.

The Saxon Catalyst

For the Celts of the sixth century AD, sex and war probably seemed like distinct experiences of life, unrelated events not linked in any way. Yet in the Celtic epic poem *Táin Bó Cualinge*, sexual behaviour had a dramatic influence on the course of war. Queen Maev used her body to entice male warriors to fight with her army and CúChulain made a formidable enemy when he refused the sexual advances of the Mórrígán. The use of sexuality to gain an advantage in battle was a Celtic paradigm, a tool used to create or destroy alliances.

After the Saxons invaded Celtic Britain, sex and war became interrelated in a different way when military reversals had an indirect effect on the sexual behaviour of the Celts. For more than a century, the bitter conflict with the Saxons severely stressed Celtic society in proportion to the distance from the fields of battle. Responding to the personal and cultural crises created by the lengthy war, many Celts altered their fundamental view of the world and their place in it, including their approach to love and sexuality. And Christianity became the vehicle shaping the change in paradigms.

Before the initial Saxon invasion of 449 AD, the Christians were a minority among the Celts, a curious sect tolerated by the druids. By the time the Saxons halted their westward expansion more than a century later, the Christians had become a dominant force in Celtic society. And Christianity permanently altered many aspects of traditional Celtic life.

*

In 449 AD, a High King of the southern British Celts named Vortigern sought the help of mercenaries in a squabble with his neighbours. He invited the Saxon warrior band of the brothers Horsa and Hengeist to fight alongside his army, offering them riches in return for their aid.[1] When the battle was done, when Vortigern's enemies were defeated, he granted British land to the Saxons as their reward. He planned to keep the foreign soldiers close at hand if he should again need their services. But the Saxons soon mutinied, complaining that their pay and living conditions were intolerable. And so began a conflict between Celt and Saxon that would endure for centuries.

Prior to the Saxon invasions, southern Britain had always been a tempting target for restless foreign intruders. Before the time of Julius Caesar's raids across the English Channel in 55-54 BC, many Celtic tribes had sailed from Gaul and Iberia to dispossess their British cousins.[2] The Roman conquest in 43 AD led by Aulus Plautius imposed a temporary external order on the quarrelsome Celtic tribes, occasionally marred by ineffective revolts against the Empire. But the Roman withdrawal of 410 AD left the Celtic clans politically disorganized, unable to mount an efficient defence of their shores. When the Saxons began to arrive in large numbers sixty years later, the Celtic tribes not immediately endangered were apathetic, allowing the invaders to establish a permanent foothold in Britain.

Under the Roman occupation, the Celtic way of life did not have to struggle to survive. The Romans were interested in political and economic dominance, not cultural supremacy. They did not tamper with the native religion, law, or tribal structure as long as these local institutions did not interfere with the objectives of the Empire. Any Celt who adopted the ways of the foreign overlords did so by choice, not by force.[3] But the Saxons represented a threat to Celtic culture beyond the previous experience of the native Britons. The invaders were hostile and violent, embracing a warrior ethic that glorified death in battle. They were not merely interested in the economic exploitation of Celtic Britain. They did not want to incorporate the native clans into their own culture through intermarriage. The objective of the Saxons was the slaughter of every Celtic man, woman and child.[4]

Unremitting warfare was the Saxon way of life. When they could find no foreign enemies, they fought among themselves with blood feuds and dynastic struggles. Life was harsh and short, with an average expectancy of thirty five years.[5] But for men who died in battle, the reward in the afterlife was great. With a religious outlook similar to the Norse, they believed that a buxom *waelcyrge* maiden would conduct the battle slain warrior to Waelheall where he would feast until the chief god Woden needed his services.[6] But the intense preoccupation with a glorious death resulted in a sombre and depressing approach to daily existence. With an almost Christian perspective, the poet of the epic poem *Beowulf* reflected on the joyless outlook of the Saxons with the observation, 'The days on earth for every one of us are numbered.'[7]

In the strict patriarchy of the Saxons, women held low status. They were little better than chattels, destined to serve men and suffer hardship in silence. Regardless of societal rank, they could be bought and sold at the whim of their husband or father. And they imperilled their life if they rejected the sexual advances of the man who controlled their destiny. When their male master died, they were sometimes killed and interred in the same grave to serve him even in death.[8] So rigid were the gender roles in Saxon society that the very notion of women bearing arms was monstrous, a storyteller's device to evoke terror in the audience.[9]

The vast cultural differences between Celt and Saxon made violent conflict inevitable. And the militaristic paradigms of the Saxons had sufficient power to break out of Vortigern's former kingdom and drive westward across Britain. At every encounter, they defeated the Celts, forcing the survivors to migrate into Wales, Ireland, and Armorica.[10] But under the leadership of the legendary warlord named Arthur, the Celts achieved a major victory over the Saxons at Badon in approximately 518 AD, temporarily halting the relentless onslaught of the invaders. The peace lasted for a generation, long enough for the Saxons to recover enough strength to continue their advance across Britain.

*

In the middle of the sixth century AD, a Celtic monk named Gildas emigrated from southern Britain to Armorica. He was a refugee, a fugitive from the unending conflicts ravaging his homeland. He was not the only Celt searching for a place of peace, for a sanctuary far from the blood and pain of battle. The Saxons had displaced thousands of native Britons who wandered through strange lands spreading the news of a genocidal war. And many had fled to Armorica, establishing a Celtic colony in the peninsula of France now known as Brittany.

When he set foot on foreign soil, Gildas was an angry and bitter man. He had been born in the year of the battle of Badon and for most of his life had enjoyed the temporary peace created by the Celtic victory. As a monk, he had devoted himself to cloistered prayer and scholarship, untroubled by the hatred smouldering between his people and the Saxons. But when the Saxons resumed their attacks on the Celts, he was forced to flee or perish.

Once he was safe in Armorica, Gildas felt compelled to purge his outrage and resentment with words, with the sole weapon at his disposal. In 560 AD, he wrote *On the Ruin of Britain* which became the only surviving eyewitness account of the early Saxon wars. In the work, he graphically testified to the massacre of the Celts by the Saxons for no purpose beyond the lust for killing.[11] The result was an enduring indictment of Saxon ethics that cannot be totally dismissed as the biased ranting of a disgruntled monk.[12]

But Gildas did not exclusively blame the Saxon invaders for the troubles afflicting his homeland. He also accused the Celtic leadership of incompetence, cowardice and petty greed for their failure to organize an effective resistance against the enemy. In all likelihood, Gildas echoed an opinion common to many of the Celts who had lost homes, friends and families to the marauding Saxons. For these men and women who now had only memories of their past life to sustain them, the fabric of their society must have seemed to be unravelling.

Traditional Celtic paradigms had not prepared people for the terrible events in southern Britain. According to the customs of the Celts war was waged against other warriors. There was no glory in slaying non-combatants. The Brehon Law protected all people, friend and foe alike. After combat, peace could be made without compromising honour. But the Saxons lived by a different vision of reality and waged war with an alien set of rules. Armed conflict was a way of life whose crowning achievement was death amid the gore of battle. They gave the enemy no quarter and expected none themselves.

When the Celts perceived the failure of their political and military institutions to repel the Saxons, they probably began to question the other paradigms of their society that they had taken for granted.[13] Displaced by war, confused by the instability created by the disintegration of family and clan, some individuals found themselves estranged from the traditions and practices of their ancestors. As they searched for new viewpoints to make sense of the unusual circumstances created by the Saxon onslaught, they were likely to closely scrutinize the philosophical, religious and moral underpinnings of their culture. Eventually, a polarization occurred. Some people clung to the old way of life while others demanded change. But others believed that the time was right for a revolution in Celtic thought, for the exchange of one set of ideas and institutions for another.[14]

A significant number of the British Celts were Christians who saw nothing unusual in the destruction caused by the Saxons. These were men and women who had already abandoned the Celtic paradigms to adopt a different vision of the world. For the Christians, the foreign invaders were merely a scourge sent by their god to punish wickedness and test their faith.[15] This notion of a judgement for sins was at the heart of the Christian religion.[16] And it was possible that many Celtic Christians also saw the Saxon carnage as an opportunity to spread their message. As their pagan neighbours groped for new paradigms to make sense of unusual events, the Chris-

tians offered a ready made explanation for the failure of traditional Celtic institutions and provided a functional alternative.

Because the Celts had a decentralized political structure,
the Christian conversion of a local clan chieftain did not guarantee the spread of the new religion. Large segments of the
population had to directly accept Christianity without coercion
from a higher civil authority. And in order for a great number
of people to adopt Christianity, there had to be a general
malaise of spirit for which the Christians offered a cure. During the sixth century AD, the Saxons stimulated a Celtic cultural crisis to varying degrees depending on the distance from
southern Britain. For the inhabitants of Kent and Sussex, the
Saxon threat was imminent and their traditional paradigms
ineffective. Their old way of life was destroyed by sword and
fire. Yet for the Celts of remote Donegal, the Saxons were a
distant danger of no immediate concern. During the sixth
century AD, the effect was to help stimulate a higher rate of
Christian conversion in areas closer to the Saxons.[17] In the
northern and western mountains of Ireland and Britain, the
traditional pagan ways endured for centuries.

Prior to the crisis created by the arrival of the Saxons,
Christianity in Ireland and Britain had to depend on persuasion and example to acquire its converts. To flourish, it could
not appear completely alien to the Celtic way of life. Despite
Christian folklore to the contrary, a pagan did not merely hear
the words of Christ and immediately adopt the new religion.
People had to be ready to change their fundamental way of life,
had to be ready to abandon family and tradition. When Christians were a minority in a culture, they were viewed as outsiders, as curious zealots devoted to a mysterious cult figure who
was shamefully executed on a cross.[18] Conversion required a
degree of dissatisfaction with an individual's spiritual status
and a willingness to explore possible alternatives. If a Christian priest told a pagan woman to abandon polyandry because
it endangered her spiritual health, her response would depend
on her state of mind at the time. If she were content with her
life and her husbands, she would scoff at the priest. But if she
was troubled by either internal or external conflict, she might

heed the Christian message as a potential solution to her personal problems.

The Christians expected a person accepting the initiation ceremony of baptism to sever the existing social relationships of family and clan, replacing them with ties to other Christians.[19] The language employed by the Christians when they called each other 'brother', 'sister', and 'father' emphasized the roles of the new family unit for converts. The Saxon wars aided the conversion process by forcibly dissolving many of the traditional social relationships binding the Celts. When a person had lost family and friends, the Christians were willing to provide a new social group to ease the pain of loss.

To become a Christian meant that a person had undergone a conversion, had cast aside old viewpoints in favour of new ones. The convert believed the ceremony of baptism represented a passage from deviance into righteousness. But for the pagan outsider, it appeared as if the convert had embraced fanaticism.[20] Nowhere was the contrast between the pagan and Christian ways of life more apparent than in the area of sexuality. In theory, the convert agreed to no longer enjoy pleasure during sex and to allow other Christians to supervise any future activities, both in and out of the bedroom. It is impossible to know with certainty the effectiveness of the baptism ceremony in changing the sexual behaviour of the Celts. Perhaps due to backsliding, perhaps due to a precarious social position, the early Celtic Christians tolerated a higher degree of sexual permissiveness when compared to the Roman sect. But for all Christians, baptism did inherently involve accepting a degree of limitation on sexual behaviour.

One of the principal tools used by the Christians to govern the conduct of their flock was shame. The Celts were no strangers to the concepts of honour and disgrace. Deeds sanctioned by Celtic society brought honour while prohibited conduct resulted in disgrace. But the Christians extended the idea of shame to include sexuality and the human body. For the convert, celibacy brought honour while sexual indulgence earned shame. The ultimate penalty for flagrant violations of the rules was expulsion from the Christian community, a formidable threat for a person who had already lost one home to the Saxons.

During the time following the collapse of the Roman Empire, the Christians provided a degree of stability in a chaotic world.[21] As the political map of Europe repeatedly changed with the influx of new peoples from the east, only the Christian institutions seemed permanent. And with their control of literacy, the Christian clergy could insure that no rival message would reach the ears of their flock. Although the Celtic Christians believed themselves an independent branch of Christianity, their ideological foundations lay in the same basic mix of Gospel, Old Testament, and philosophic writings as their religious competitors in Rome or Byzantium. Certain that they alone held a monopoly on truth, the seized the opportunity created by the Saxon wars to spread their beliefs among their fellow Celts.

Spiritual Warriors

Around the time the Saxons first began to challenge Celtic society, the Christians introduced the monastic system into Britain and Ireland. The ideal of the lonely spiritual warrior who abandoned family and friends to battle for salvation in remote landscapes appealed to the Celtic sense of the heroic. The monasteries provided a peaceful refuge from the personal and military conflicts beyond their walls. And as the monasteries grew in status and influence, their connection with the monastic centres of continental Europe funnelled Roman Christian ideas and viewpoints into Celtic society.

Although the Celts enthusiastically embraced the monastic system, its origins lay far from the temperate shores of Britain and Ireland. The ascetic movement was born in the eastern Mediterranean, in the barren deserts of Egypt. This remote fringe of the Roman Empire was the cradle of Christianity, the land where the infant religion was nurtured until it was strong enough to replace the traditional beliefs of Rome itself. But to survive its formative years, Christianity had to compete with Isis, Mithra, and other established forms of worship popular in the Middle East. Shrewdly, the early Christians borrowed concepts from their rivals. From the Gnostics, they adopted the idea that only spirituality had importance.[1] From the Manicheans and Stoics, they took a distrust of sexuality.[2] And from the example of autocratic power in the eastern kingdoms, they embraced a rigid hierarchy granting supreme authority to a bishop or abbot.

Many of the early Egyptian Christians focused on mystical spirituality, rejecting the material world. They sought martyrdom as an easy entry into heaven and the usually tolerant Roman government was happy to offer dissident Christians a painful death.[3] But as the Christian belief grew more established and less persecuted, martyrdom became increasingly hard to find. So the mystics turned their backs on everyday life and sought a living martyrdom, a self-imposed ritual of daily suffering and deprivation.[4] The first Christian ascetics left the Nile Valley, retreating to the desert to starve, pray and sometimes hallucinate. In the stark expanse of sand and stone, they could be alone with themselves and with their mystical visions. Most of these hermits were men who perceived themselves as warriors battling with Satan for the mastery of their bodies and their souls.[5] And they took great pride in their life of privation. A dying martyr suffered only a brief moment to gain the pleasure of heaven. But for the ascetic, each day was a torture, each moment a perpetual martyrdom. It was an intensely self-centred existence. The rest of the world could be damned while the hermit remained intent on his own private salvation.[6]

Roman observers recorded the churlish manners and abhorrent hygiene of the desert dwelling Christians. The hermits never bathed. They were indifferent to the length of their hair and to the trim of their nails. Vermin scuttled across their emaciated bodies. They hurled stones and curses at any curiosity seeker bold enough to disturb their solitude.[7] But the ascetics believed that this rude squalor was the only path to eternal life. And their poor attitude towards personal cleanliness permeated the monastic movement for centuries afterwards.

Eventually, the desolation of the empty desert proved too oppressive a burden for many hermits. They formed monasteries so their lonely struggles could be brightened by the occasional glimpse of another human being who shared their beliefs. In the first communities, each monk lived and prayed apart from the others, coming together only for a common meal or service. The early monasteries of Egypt were collections of caves, crude stone huts, or shallow pits etched from the soil.[8]

Although the Egyptian hermits fled to the desert to escape

the increasing worldliness of the organized Christian church, they found themselves in need of an internal structure of their own. A community of maverick monks could not function smoothly without rules governing their interaction with one another. A former Roman soldier named Pachomius provided the first regulations for the Egyptian monasteries. He envisioned each community as a legion of monks modelled on a military basis, bound together by discipline and allegiance to an abbot who displayed the leadership qualities of a general.[9] This system appealed to hermits who believed they were spiritual warriors struggling against Satan and their own flesh. Together, the ascetics of the desert vowed to wage a united struggle against the forces of darkness seeking to doom their souls. And if a man faltered in his resolve, his comrades were near at hand to bolster his strength. Pachomius created a new kind of warrior sodality, a fraternity sworn to fight battles in a supernatural realm. But the warrior-monks did not limit themselves to mystical weapons to achieve their objectives.

The Egyptian ascetics were not beyond direct intervention in the politics of the world they claimed to have abandoned. On one occasion, an organized army of ill-smelling hermits invaded the city of Alexandria. They took prisoner the bishop of the city, threatening him with death until he declared heretical the works of the Christian philosopher, Origen.[10]

The hatred of the Egyptian monks towards Origen was itself remarkable. He was a scholar of Alexandria who remained in the city but lived the life of an ascetic. He slept little and ate poorly. As an added show of devotion to the ideal of chastity, he cut off his penis as a teenager so he could never succumb to the temptations of his own flesh.[11] In his writings, he attempted to make the Christian doctrines more acceptable to educated pagans of the Roman upper class. Prior to Origen's time, Christianity had been largely a criminal activity of the plebs, practised by slaves and the downtrodden in the mystical hope of attaining a better life after death. Origen gave Christian thought a degree of intellectual respectability by using Greek philosophical concepts to analyse Christian spirituality in allegorical terms.

Origen stressed that many of the fantastic events in scripture were parables to emphasize a moral point and did not actually occur.[12] But the unwashed monks of the desert objected strenuously to this position. God and Satan had to be real beings for these men who had abandoned their entire lives to struggle against the spirit of darkness. If all scripture was merely an allegory of good and evil, the suffering endured by the monks for its own sake would be shorn of merit.

Surrounded by wild-eyed fanatics who feared no earthly authority, the bishop of Alexandria relented. He declared Origen's ideas a heretical deviation. And the warrior-monks returned to their hovels in the desert, remaining ever vigilant for deeds or ideas that would diminish the religious significance of their lifestyle.

Eventually, news of the monastic movement reached the shores of Europe, popularized in part by the *Life of Antony* written by Bishop Athanasius of Alexandria. This book outlined the idealized adventures of a desert hermit and enjoyed a wide circulation among Christian scholars.[13] It inspired Martin of Tours to establish one of the first European monastic communities at Marmoutier in Gaul.

Born in 315 AD, Martin was the son of a Roman soldier whose legion embraced Christianity a year after his birth. When he grew to manhood, Martin became a cavalry officer in the armies of Emperor Constantine II.[14] After retiring from military service, he studied under Hilary of Poitiers, the Gaulish Celt who contributed greatly to the Christian doctrine of the trinity. Through Hilary's influence, Martin became thoroughly familiar with the Celtic concept of a tripartite god as it applied to Christianity. Because this doctrine divided the Christian God into the aspects of Father, Son, and Holy Ghost, it assured the divinity of Christ.[15] Adopted by the Roman Christians, the trinity idea was used to combat Arianism which ascribed divinity only to the Father in heaven.

Initially, Martin did not set out to establish a monastery. By 350 AD, the Christian diocesan system was fully in place in Gaul, a direct copy of the Roman scheme of provincial administration. Almost all of the bishops were bureaucrats and landlords, more concerned with finances than faith. The leaders of the new religion had grown corrupt and torpid, violently opposing any threat to the status quo.[16] Repelled by the corruption he perceived among the Christian clergy, Martin retreated from the world to a place of private worship at Marmoutier on the outskirts of Tours. Other people were soon impressed by his piety and came to speak with the holy hermit. Some men stayed, convinced that Martin had a remedy for the soul damaging decay they saw around them. These newcomers built huts near Martin's cell, creating a loosely knit community.[17]

Martin was a former officer of the Emperor's legions and he could not help but lead the men who looked to him for spiritual guidance. He organized the monks of Marmoutier as if they were a disciplined military unit, swearing them to the ascetic ideal and demanding obedience to his rule. Then he gave them a mission beyond prayer and privation for the sake of salvation. He ordered the monks to wander the countryside, desecrating pagan places of worship and tearing down the remaining symbols of druid belief which was still popular among the Celts of Gaul. This roving band of fanatics did not hesitate to use physical force to achieve their objectives, terrorizing any man or woman who clung to pre-Christian beliefs.

Martin may have sent his warrior-monks into battle against the remnants of druid practice in Gaul at the order of the Emperor Gratian.[18] Under the influence of Ambrose of Milan, Gratian had revoked official Roman tolerance of all religions except Christianity, reversing a centuries old tradition. If Martin was obeying Imperial orders, Gratian was indeed shrewd. Without close supervision from the head of government, Martin's warrior-monk sodality could easily have become an unpredictable force with the potential to challenge the theocratic union of Christianity and Empire.

By grafting Roman military perspectives onto the mysticism of the Egyptian ascetics, Martin created a new vision of the monastic role which would influence European monks for a thousand years. While Martin's followers remained predominantly concerned with their own salvation, they were not hermits and they interacted regularly with the secular com-

munities around them. Teaching, proselytizing, and influenc-
ing local politics, the European monks sought to shape the
affairs of the world.

Severius chronicled Martin's exploits in *The Life of Martin*.
The tale was similar to a Celtic saga, complete with adventures
and miracles and triumph against overwhelming odds. In the
fifth century AD, Severius' work circulated widely in Ireland
and Britain. The story of a soldier who defied corrupt authority
to set his own path through life appealed to the Celts and
helped persuade them to establish their own monasteries.[19] As
a result, Martin of Tours is often called the 'Father of Celtic
Monasticism'.

The writings of John Cassian gave further encouragement
to the monastic movement among the Celts. Between 385 AD
and 390 AD, he visited the hermit communities of Syria and
Egypt and believed the ascetic lifestyle would have universal
appeal for Christians. Afterwards he lived for a time at the
monastery of Lérins, observing the European monks.[20] This
community was founded on a group of small Mediterranean
islands off Cannes by Honoratus, a Roman raised in Britain.
Eventually Cassian went to Hippo where he died in 430 AD.

Like their Egyptian contemporaries, Cassian, Honoratus,
and the other European monks were also troubled by Christian
thinkers whose ideas threatened their way of life. On the
surface, Augustine's notions of grace and original sin were
opposed to the hermit's belief that virtue sprang from inside
himself. If good works had no value, if salvation came directly
from God in the form of 'grace', there was no point to suffering
intense deprivation. But the writings of Cassian reconciled
original sin with the ascetic lifestyle by claiming that 'grace'
was a gift given to those who earned it.[21] Cassian's logic led to
a Pelagian conclusion by granting men and women a degree of
control over their destinies. But his works escaped official
censure and became the fundamental philosophical basis for
European monasteries. In Egypt, the hallmark of the monastic
movement was its isolation from society. Hermits shut themselves away from the world to save the only soul that had any
importance – their own. The European monasteries were also

devoted to refuge from the Roman Empire, from the barbarians who overcame it, and from the mundane problems of everyday life. But the European monks were more willing to associate with outsiders, particularly if local events threatened to disrupt their private struggles.

*

For the Greeks and early Romans, physical beauty was important. To improve their appearance, they used cosmetics and exercised extensively. Their art emphasized the magnificence of the human form. Anyone disfigured by disease or accident was a social outcast. And any infant unlucky enough to be born with a visible defect was exposed to die in the wilderness. But the Christian ascetics rejected delight in the human body, developing a hatred for the flesh and all its urges. They focused their attention on the self, on the inner being imprisoned by a shell of skin and bone. Joy in the splendour of the world and in male and female bodies depended on external stimuli which distracted the monk from his quest for salvation.[22] In order for the monks to subdue their fundamental human sexuality, they had to replace enjoyment of the body with pain and suffering.

The ascetics did not need Augustine's convoluted logic to develop an aversion to sex. In the monastic paradigm, chastity was linked with solitude. A sexual relationship established a communication with another person when partners shared their innermost feelings and reactions. The monks exclusively reserved such intimate activity for Christ and later for Mary, the idealized vision of Christian femininity. To avoid sexual encounters, the monks had to remain alone as much as possible. And if circumstances forced a monk into the company of others, he had to be supervised at all times.

Since sexuality brought pleasure, it was incompatible with an ethic that embraced misery. But the hermits did not fully understand that desire came from within themselves. They believed that evil spirits caused their bodies to respond sexually to a person or thought.[23] Like hunger, like weariness, lust was an urge induced by demons to betray the soul.

In the Egyptian desert, the monks attempted to control their
sexuality through dietary restrictions. Surviving on meagre
rations for long periods of time, they believed that malnourish-
ment would suppress their sexual drive. But their desires were
irrepressible and continued to trouble both the hungry monk
and the well fed novices newly arrived in the monasteries.[24]
When the rare woman did enter the desert, she became an
immediate object of sexual fascination, evoking thoughts the
hermit had struggled vigorously to repress. To seduce any
females that came their way, the unwashed and bedraggled
monks would use sweet words. If that failed, some monks
balled their fists and satisfied themselves with violent rape.
Young boys were also at risk of molestation in the Egyptian
monastic communities. Assuming that their sons were protected by their gender, many widowers came to the desert with
their male children. And these youths immediately became the
object of the older monks' sexual desires.[25]

Ideally, a monk would chastise himself for sexual lapses
without depending on his comrades to bring the matter to his
attention. It was not unusual for monks to burn themselves
with hot coals or place sharp thorns against their genitals in
response to fleeting sexual thoughts. But if the monastic community discovered that an individual monk succumbed to his
sexual desire, he was not banished in disgrace.[26] Instead, he
was given a formal punishment involving self-inflicted pain
administered under supervision.

Although the concept of sadomasochistic sexuality did not
exist in the early Christian era, the constant linking of pain
with sex probably induced a masochistic sexual response in
some ascetics. It was possible for self-administered punishment to itself become a sexual stimulus, possibly even leading
to orgasm. While the occurrence of masochistic sexuality was
not recorded, it was within the range of potential human
responses for the cloistered monks.

In Gaul, dietary restrictions could not be regularly used to
combat sexual desire. Martin's monks were engaged in physical combat with pagan worshippers. And monks who skir-
mished with enemies of flesh and bone had to eat well to

maintain their strength. As Martin's zealots wandered the countryside, numerous opportunities for sexual adventures must have arisen.

Because the European monasteries were generally not as isolated as their Egyptian counterparts, the monks had to develop a more strict code of behaviour to insure chastity. Once a man entered the monastic community, the watchful eyes of his comrades were always upon him. He could not leave the confines of the monastery unless accompanied by a group of monks. The door of his cell had to remain open so he could not masturbate in privacy.[27]

Homosexuality was glibly called a 'special friendship'. The rules of each monastery to govern the behaviour of the monks contained various physical punishments to deter homosexual activity. Usually, any outward display of affection of one man for another was disciplined as severely as the sexual act itself. Even such innocent practices as tucking a tunic around the thighs while washing clothes was prohibited as a potential source of temptation for another.[28] Nocturnal emissions were also a source of concern for the monks. To explain the uncontrollable dreams that brought such intense pleasure, they invented the succubus, a beautiful female demon who tempted men in their sleep. To ward against her attentions, monks would tie a metal crucifix to their genitals before retiring for the night. The custom originated in the Roman arena where gladiators tied bits of cold metal to their testicles the night before combat.[29] They believed that the chill of the metal would prevent an involuntary nocturnal ejaculation which would sap their strength.

In his writings, John Cassian recognized the difficulty of imposing chastity on monks in a well populated European environment. He believed that the tendency to fornicate was rooted in the body and only physical chastisement could overcome the urge. At the time he wrote, the Christians termed as fornication all unsanctioned sexual acts.[30] The distinction between adultery and fornication did not arise until Augustine used the term adultery to describe any sexual activity infringing on the marriage vows.

Cassian identified three groups of sexual acts threatening a monk's spiritual welfare. He mentioned fornication where two individuals join, fornication without contact with another, and fornication of thought. The prohibition against sexual thoughts had the most far reaching impact, since few people could pass a day without even a brief sexual image passing through their mind. This restriction even included thoughts of a mother or sister since they could lead a man to think of another woman or worse, to fantasize an incestuous union. Cassian believed that a dedicated monk could eventually achieve a neuter state of non-sexuality after years of administering pain in response to sexual thoughts.

Although much paper and ink was used to advise a man how to remain chaste, the sexuality of women ascetics was largely ignored. The Christians admitted that women possessed souls like men but the traditional paradigms of the Mediterranean patriarchies hampered the early establishment of exclusively female ascetic communities independent of male supervision. Initially, Christians encouraged women who wanted to embrace virginity to live at home, tending to the domestic needs of fathers, brothers and other male relatives. Male clerics who did address female virginity stressed the risk of childbirth and the dominance of an ill-tempered husband to make chastity more attractive to women. The Christian priesthood was composed of men who assumed that a woman who merely chose celibacy would never again have a sexual thought or desire.[31] Their attitude demonstrated a lack of communication between the genders common to the Mediterranean cultures of the period.

The anti-sexual doctrines developed by Augustine in the early part of the fifth century AD found a natural home in the communities of ascetic monks. As monasteries sprouted across the landscape of Europe, the monks used Augustine's logic to defend their sexually repressive ideas. They believed chastity was a more perfect state of being and expected a degree of sexual discipline from all Christians.

*

The archives of Leyden contain a much disputed document claiming that Gaulish monks fled to untroubled Ireland during the turmoil created by the collapse of the Roman Empire.[32] It is doubtful that these refugees were responsible for starting the early Irish monasteries. All other records indicated that the native Celts introduced the monastic system after witnessing the lifestyle of the Gaulish monks during visits to Marmoutier and Lérins. Along with their personal observations, the Celtic Christians brought home copies of *The Life of Antony* and *The Life of Martin* to serve as textbooks for the operation of a monastery.

But the Christian Celts of Ireland and Britain did more than merely borrow the basic concept of the monastery as a retreat from a corrupt world. They added their own cultural perspective to the monastic system, creating a focus which went beyond prayer, suffering, and chastity. The earliest Celtic monasteries were also devoted to learning. And as centuries passed, the Christian monks of Ireland and Britain gained a virtual monopoly on knowledge both holy and profane.

Prior to the arrival of Christianity, the druids had developed a tradition of learning in their own schools. Any person who wished to become a druid had to undergo a lengthy period of education under the supervision of an experienced teacher.[33] The subject matter was not limited to spiritual concerns since they believed that all knowledge complemented spirituality. From these druid schools, the Celtic Christians inherited a cultural paradigm linking the religious life with scholarship.

In the Christian rivalry with druid belief, the secret of writing was a potent weapon. The pre-Christian Celts depended solely on memory and the spoken word to transfer information. In the fourth century AD, the druids devised a runic script called *ogham* based on the Latin alphabet. Observation of the Roman system of writing in Britain probably stimulated the development of this proto-alphabet. Each letter was represented by a series of horizontal and vertical strokes carved in stone. Although none have survived, it is possible they also etched the runes on staves of wood, the magic wand of druid legend.[34] Named after trees and shrubs, the runes had primarily a religious significance and did not appear to convey complex information. When the educated Celts saw the Christian scrawl that spoke of great deeds and profound ideas, they were fascinated. They flocked to the monasteries to learn the art of writing, causing literacy to spread with remarkable speed throughout Ireland and Britain.

Initially, writing and reading were taught only in Latin. This became the secret language of the Christians, steeped in mystery like the *ogham* of the druids. It enabled the monks and priests to communicate with each other in a way beyond the understanding of average people.[35] It was the medium through which the great magic of Christ's message was revealed. The initiates to the wonders of the written word became known as the *fer-legham*, the men of reading. Gradually, they usurped the high social status held by the wise men and women of the druid belief.

Ninian was the first person in Britain to found a monastery with a scholastic focus. In the late fourth century AD, he journeyed to Rome and on his way home he stopped to observe Martin's community at Marmoutier. According to legend, Martin lent Ninian the services of stone masons to construct a monastery at Whithorn in Strathclyde. Ninian painted the building white and it became known as Candida Casa, the White House.[36] Whithorn developed into a great centre of learning, educating students such as Finian of Moville who later established their own monasteries.

By 600 AD, Ireland had a large number of monasteries located mostly in the central and southern part of the island. In Britain, the monasteries were built beyond the fringes of the Saxon conquests. While prayer, privation, and penance lay at the core of monastic life, the Celtic ascetics also focused on learning and education. Students flocked to Iona, Bangor, Whithorn and the other Celtic monasteries to gain knowledge of classical literature and the art of writing. Monastic archives and libraries grew until they became vast repositories of Celtic, Greek and Roman heritage. Beginning in the seventh century AD, the monks of Ireland and Britain took their tradition of scholarship and fanned out over Europe. They were credited with founding communities in France, Germany, Switzerland, and Italy. Their efforts helped to preserve the works of classical authors on the Continent and kindle the Carolingean Renaissance. But not all of the Celts embraced a monastic system that emphasized scholarship over suffering.

The western islets of Ireland are bleak, windswept, and inhospitable. To their rocky shores came the Christian men who wanted to closely imitate the hardships endured by the monks of the Egyptian desert. At Inishboffin, Inishfree, and Skellig Michael they built crude huts of stone, scant protection against the bitter Atlantic winds. They fished and scratched the stony soil to raise meagre crops.[37] And always they prayed and suffered in hope of gaining bliss in a life after death.

The growth of the monastic system in Ireland and Britain during the sixth and seventh centuries AD had a direct influence on the viewpoints of both pagan and Christian Celts. Monasteries became so abundant that a person could scarcely walk for a few hours without encountering a group of monks tilling a field or tending cattle. And the Christian ascetics were always willing to speak of their doctrines, certain that only they knew the truth about life, love, and sexuality.

Columcille

In 561 AD, a great battle was fought in Ireland known as *Cúl Dreimne*, the Battle of the Books. Both armies were composed of mixed pagan and Christian troops. Cowled monks and robed druids allied themselves with each side, hurling invisible missiles of prayer and vehement curse. When the battle was done, the blood of Christians could not be distinguished from the blood of pagans.

The leader of one army at *Cúl Dreimne* was the Christian abbot, Columcille. His name was given to him at baptism and meant 'Dove of the Church'. But he was born as Crimthan, the Wolf.[1] And his willingness to shed the blood of his kinsmen and enemies alike proved he was well named at birth.

Opposed to Columcille was Diarmuit, the High King of Ireland. He had mustered his clan to enforce a royal edict which Columcille refused to obey. He was a pagan, but he had no quarrel with the Christians. On the day of battle, he employed both druid and Christian magic, but none of the spells cast by his priests and shamans proved very effective.

Most accounts agreed that *Cúl Dreimne* was fought to maintain the right of the High King to enforce his laws. A while before the battle, Columcille had visited the abbot Finian at the monastery of Moville. For many nights he would remain awake, secretly copying a book that Finian had brought with him from Whithorn. Some sources claimed that Columcille copied the Bible.[2] Other historians believed the work was *The Gospel of St. Martin*. Whatever book so intrigued Columcille, Finian eventually discovered the deceit of his guest and demanded the copy Columcille had made. But Columcille refused and fled into the night before Finian could order his monks to take possession of the unauthorized copy by force.

Not willing to let the matter rest, Finian appealed to Diarmuit for a judgement. And after considering the issues, Diarmuit proclaimed 'to every cow belongs its calf and to every book belongs its copy.'[3] He ordered Columcille to turn the copied book over to Finian.

In the Celtic tradition, Columcille identified with his mother's family, tracing his lineage to the royal house of clan ó Donnell. But on his father's side, he was an Uí Néill, directly descended from the king and statesman, Niall of the Nine Hostages. Diarmuit was a kinsman of Columcille and head of the clan Uí Néill. But the ó Donnells did not recognize the right of the upstart Uí Néill to hold the high kingship of Ireland. So Columcille felt he was justified in defying Diarmuit's decree. Fleeing to the ó Donnell stronghold in Donegal, he announced that 'the wrong decision of a judge is a raven's call to battle.'[4]

An alternative version of the underlying cause of the battle of *Cúl Dreimne* claimed that Columcille used bell, book, and candle to curse Diarmuit for violating Christian sanctuary.[5] As a pagan, Diarmuit could not understand why the law of the land should not apply in the plots of earth inhabited by Christian clerics. Perhaps Diarmuit feared the curse of a man like Columcille who was adept at the foreign magic of the Christians. Perhaps he was angered when the malediction of a prominent ó Donnell challenged the efficient management of his Uí Néill government. Whatever the actual cause of *Cúl Dreimne*, by 561 AD sufficient friction existed between a Christian abbot and a pagan High King for a pitched battle to take place between them.

Although *Cúl Dreimne* was not fought over religious issues, it did demonstrate the growing power of the warrior-monks in Ireland. Once they were firmly established in Celtic society, Christians were not as tolerant of rival beliefs as the druids. Powerful abbots like Columcille wanted to impose a Christian vision of justice and morality to rule the land, demanding that the state acknowledge the superiority of the church. And the Christians were gradually becoming more bold in their confrontation with traditional Celtic institutions and paradigms, urging their followers to defy civil authority when it conflicted with Christian beliefs.

Unfortunately for Diarmuit, he did not channel the energy of Columcille's warrior-monks as cleverly as the Emperor Gratian did with Martin. Diarmuit did not recognize the danger to his rule posed by the warrior sodalities of Christian ascetics lurking in the many monasteries of his realm. A wiser king would have focused the worldly battle spirit of the monks towards some politically impotent scapegoat.

Columcille won the day at *Cúl Dreimne*, but he did not enjoy the fruits of his victory. Written by an ó Donnell in 1532 AD, *Betha Colaim Chille* claimed that Columcille felt deep remorse when he saw the slaughter caused by his pride.[7] He vowed to leave Ireland, to become a White Martyr living out his remaining days in foreign lands. But Columcille was probably forced into exile by the Synod of Teltown, a meeting of loyal Uí Néill clergy summoned by Diarmuit. At this gathering, Columcille was almost excommunicated from the Christian spiritual community for his theft by copy of Finian's book. He was saved only by the eloquence of his friend, Brendan of Birr, who convinced the Synod to impose banishment as a substitute punishment.[8]

By the sixth century AD, the concept of the White Martyr had taken firm hold of the Celtic Christian imagination. Monks and abbots had usurped the social position of the *áes-dana*, enjoying all the status and prestige once held by the wise men and women of the druid belief. But many ascetics rejected the praise and deference offered to them by their Christian countrymen. The only way a monk could escape social prominence was to journey to a land where he was unknown and unappreciated. Unlike the Red Martyr of blood and sharp pain, the White Martyr suffered daily the pangs of loss for family and friends he would never see again.[9]

Before leaving Ireland, Columcille gathered twelve disciples to form the nucleus of a new monastery. It was the custom of both Christian and druid spiritual leaders to surround themselves with students. In imitation of Christ, the Christians fixed the number of followers at twelve.[10] Columcille himself had been one of the twelve disciples of Finian of Clonard. This group was known as the Twelve Apostles of Ireland and included such prominent Christian leaders as Brendan the Navigator and Ciarán, the founder of the monastery at Clonmacnoise.

With his companions, Columcille embarked on the Irish sea in coracles in 565 AD. As if he were a druid, he abandoned himself to the elements, letting the random ocean winds dictate his course. Eventually the frail boats made of hide and rope landed on the island of Iona off the coast of northern Scotland. Rocky and isolated, yet with several acres of tillable pasture land, Iona must have seemed the perfect location for a monastery. Possibly, the druid tradition of locating religious colleges on islands influenced Columcille's site selection.[11] Legend claimed that Columcille's first act when he came ashore was to build the *Carn cúl rí Eirin,* the Cairn of the Back Turned on Ireland.

Iona lay in the territory controlled by clan Dál Riata. Two centuries before the arrival of Columcille, they had fled Ireland to escape a famine and the warlike clan Uí Néill. The Dál Riata came to Scotland, battling with the native Picts to establish a foothold in the new land. But they never achieved a permanent peace with the Picts and the war continued from one generation to the next.

When Columcille set foot on Iona, Conall was the king of the Dál Riata. Although he was Columcille's cousin, he bore no friendship for clan ó Donnell or clan Uí Néill.[12] The High King of Ireland continued to extract tribute from the Dál Riata, claiming sovereignty over this Irish outpost in Scotland. And he enforced his taxation with threats of invasion. Conall dared not defy his Irish overlord. Two years before Columcille's arrival he had lost a major battle with the Picts who were eager to regain the lands occupied by the Irish immigrants. Conall did not have sufficient men at arms to defend both the northern marches against the Picts and the sea coast against clan Uí Néill and clan ó Donnell.

When Conall died, the people of Dál Riata asked Columcille to crown their new king, Aeden the Wily. Initially, Aeden displayed only contempt for Columcille. Perhaps he recognized the threat to his rule implicit in a community of warrior-monks residing in his lands. Perhaps he merely did not like the arrogant and overbearing cleric who had washed up on his shores. Hoping to discredit Columcille, he offered his daughter to warm the abbot's cold bed. Columcille spurned the attentions of the princess. But he wisely complimented her on her great beauty.

Eventually, Columcille played on Aeden's fears to gain the royal grant of Iona, bullying the king with renewed threats of invasion and Christian ceremony interpreted as magic.[13] He established a monastery on the island which was to play a pivotal role in the spread of Celtic Christianity to the northern kingdoms of Saxon Britain. And from this base of operations, he embarked on a missionary expedition to the Pictish kingdom ruled by Brude mac Maelchon from his Inverness stronghold.

A later abbot of Iona named Adomnán wrote *The Life of Columcille* a century after Columcille's death. He based his work on a lost manuscript by Cuimíne Ailbe who became abbot of Iona in 657 AD.[14] Adomnán chronicled Columcille's mission to Brude, emphasizing the many battles of magic between the Christians and the druids. Columcille managed to subdue all physical and spiritual opposition, even an attack on his party by the serpentine monster of Loch Ness. As a result of his efforts, the Picts adopted Christianity.

From the accounts of Columcille's journey to Inverness, he conducted himself as if he were the leader of a military expedition. He had to conduct his party of Christian monks and Pictish interpreters through a rugged landscape inhabited by hostile pagans. In the event of a skirmish, he could look to no ally for aid. But Columcille's followers were warrior-monks, bound by discipline and their devotion to an ideal. It mattered little to them that their weapons were spiritual, unable to wound or kill. The foolhardy venture pitting so few men against an entire nation must have astonished the Picts.

After Columcille returned to Iona, the Picts remained Christian. Perhaps this was because Columcille did not merely offer the Picts an exchange of Christian magic for druid. The monks of his party were all well educated, acquainted with advanced techniques of agriculture, husbandry and metallurgy. Columcille may well have bartered his practical knowledge in exchange for the conversion of King Brude and his court.

In 575 AD, Ae mac Ainmire convened the Convention of Drumceat. With this shrewd political gesture, the new High King of Ireland hoped to achieve a consensus among his followers to levy further tribute on the clan Dál Riata. As a secondary objective, he wanted to limit the power of the bards who heaped ridicule on him with their skilful satires.

To attend this convention as the representative of the Dál Riata, Columcille returned to Ireland. This was a clear choice of delegates on the part of King Aeden. The Dál Riata were now Columcille's adopted Christian flock, yet he enjoyed enormous prestige among the ó Donnells and the other clans who chaffed under the rule of the Uí Néill High Kings. In addition, Columcille was himself a member of the bards' guild and could hurl barbed satires with vexing precision. He also made frequent use of the curse, the verbal prediction of harm which would befall his enemies.

Later Christian legend made various excuses for Columcille's flagrant violation of the ethic of the White Martyr. Some tales claimed that the Angel Axal granted him dispensation from his vows to return to Ireland. Another story claimed that he kept his face buried in his cowl so he would look upon no man or woman of his native land.[15] One apologist asserted that he tied clods of Scottish turf to his sandals so he never actually set foot in Ireland.[16] Apparently, Columcille believed that the political advantage to be gained by reducing the tribute of the Dál Riata and defending the society of bards outweighed his pledge of lifelong exile. And he left the matter of his vow for posterity to sort out.

At Drumceat, the question of tribute was quickly decided. Since an overseas campaign larger than a raid would strain too many Irish resources, clan Dál Riata was granted its independence. But the issue of the bards was more complex. By the time of the Convention of Drumceat, many of the higher ranks of society were Christian. Priests were gradually usurping the functions of the bards, resenting the traditional poets who glorified the pre-Christian heritage of the Celts. The Christian clergy would like nothing better than to replace the bards as the only officially recognized storytellers.

Perhaps to annoy the Uí Néill High King, perhaps to avenge the judgement against him by rival Christians at Teltown, Columcille spoke in defence of the bards. According to legend, he held aloft a skull and reminded the gathering that only the bardic songs kept honour alive after flesh had withered from bone.[17] After hearing the words of Columcille, the Convention agreed not to eliminate the bards from Irish society. But they did curtail the power of the traditional poets by requiring that they labour only for a single patron. In this way, bards were less likely to turn stinging satires against the person who provided their livelihood.

Columcille died in 597 AD in his monastery at Iona. He left no writings of his own, no clue to his innermost thoughts. Christian legend portrayed him as a spiritual man, intent on his own private salvation. But throughout his career, he manoeuvred his monks as if he were the chieftain of a warrior sodality intent on conquest. He sent his followers into battle against the swords of Diarmuit Uí Néill and the magic of Brude mac Maelchon. During his residence in the kingdom of the Dál Riata, he was an unpredictable force, sometimes aiding and sometimes thwarting the ambitions of the king. In the style of the Celtic abbot, he freely interfered with local politics to gain an advantage for himself or his followers.

Despite the large body of fact and legend devoted to Columcille's adventures, little was mentioned about his attitude towards sexuality. In one piece of folklore, a Christian man came to Columcille complaining that his wife would no longer share his bed. Columcille offered the wife a choice between the duty of sex with her husband and the enforced chastity of a nunnery. After hearing this, the wife relented and once more embraced her husband.[18]

This story showed that Columcille viewed sex as a responsibility of marriage and little more. If the sexual duty could not be fulfilled, then celibacy was the only available alternative for a Christian. Under the pre-Christian paradigms of the Celts, a woman who no longer enjoyed the attentions of her husband would merely choose another lover. By the time of Columcille, divorce was no longer an option for Christians. Although he displayed the attributes of a Christianized druid, Columcille's sexual attitudes appeared to be strongly influenced by the ascetic viewpoints of the monastery.

Columcille seemed to live in an exclusively male world. On the rare occasions when he did interact with women, he ignored their passions and aspirations, treating them as objects. He had little difficulty refusing the offer of Aeden's daughter or sending a woman to a convent.

The legendary tale of the Crane of Drumceat also demonstrated Columcille's disdain for women. At the Convention of Drumceat, the High King's wife frequently troubled Columcille, publicly challenging his central position among the delegates from Dál Riata. She advised her husband to be rid of the ambitious cleric who was skinny as a crane. To punish her impudence, Columcille used Christian magic to transform her into a crane doomed to endlessly wander the earth.[19] Presumably, if Columcille had been insulted by a man, he would have responded with sharp words or drawn sword. But when ridiculed by a woman, he took particular delight in permanently distorting her body, rendering her sexless.

Personal power was the central focus of Columcille's life. The thrill of command and the flush of victory seemed to consume his thoughts and guide his actions, leaving little energy for a personal struggle with repressed sexuality. When Aeden's daughter tempted him, he weighed sexual adventure against political gain. And he rejected the princess.

After Columcille's death, the abbots of Iona continued to acquire power and prestige among the Celts and the Saxon invaders to the south. For several centuries, the monks interfered with local politics directly and indirectly. To emphasize the supremacy of religion over the state, the abbots crowned the kings of Dál Riata and buried them in the graveyard of Iona.[20] When expedient, they sheltered political refugees and sent envoys to whisper intrigue in the ears of Saxon kings. In major wars and petty feuds, they took sides, seeking to enhance the influence of the Celtic Christians. But when the Viking longships repeatedly raided Iona in the ninth century AD, the monks had to flee, abandoning their island for the safety of the inland Irish monastery at Kells.

*

Columcille was a transitional figure during a time of shifting Celtic sexual paradigms. He guarded his own sexuality in accordance with the Christian code for celibates, but he did not appear greatly concerned with the sexual behaviour of others. He also retained many of the behavioural characteristics of a druid *áes-dana*, commanding the elements, casting spells and engaging in mystical battles. He seemed intent on acquiring personal power and prestige by successfully challenging the political institutions of the Celts, indirectly benefiting the entire Christian community. Possibly he was reluctant to simultaneously tamper with the fundamental paradigms of Celtic sexuality, wary of a backlash which might erode his growing political influence.

Perhaps Columcille merely reflected the fluctuating beliefs of the society in which he lived. By the year of his death, much of Britain was under Saxon control. British Celts had fled to strongholds in Wales, Cornwall and Scotland. Their future appeared grim. And Christianity was growing more bold, openly challenging the traditional Celtic beliefs and way of life. Columcille appeared to be merely a typical Celt of the tumultuous times, unsure if he were a druid, unsure if he were a Roman Christian.

Columbanus

While Columcille laboured to expand his political power and influence from his island base at Iona, another prominent Christian chose the White Martyrdom of permanent exile. His name was Columbanus and he would ultimately spread the Celtic vision of Christianity far beyond the rocky shores of Britain and Ireland. In legend, the exploits of the two men sometimes overlapped. When the Anglo-Norman English eventually gained political mastery over all of the Celtic lands, they anglicized the name Columcille, calling him Columba the Elder. Columbanus they dubbed Columba the Younger. This created confusion as later medieval chroniclers attributed the deeds of one man to the other. But only in legend was there any direct connection between the two monks.[1]

Columbanus received his Latin name at baptism. Early in his life, he donned the monk's cowl, studying first at Sinell's monastery at Lough Erne in Ireland. Later he moved to the larger Christian monastic school at Bangor founded by Comgall.[2] The materials available for study in these monasteries were not censored by any Christian zealot who believed that secular knowledge was a threat to spirituality. Columbanus probably received an education in astronomy, mathematics, general philosophy and the classical works of Rome and Greece.[3] His later writings revealed a degree of familiarity with these subjects as well as fluency in Greek and Latin.

In 591 AD, Columbanus decided to leave Ireland. He was forty-seven years old, an advanced age for such a bold undertaking in an era when disease and hardship claimed lives early. But unlike Columcille, he chose to voyage to France, to a distant land populated by foreigners who spoke an alien tongue. With the customary twelve followers, he sailed for the country once known as Gaul.

Long before Columbanus' arrival, the Franks had invaded Gaul. By force of arms, their king Clovis established a great empire extending throughout modern France into Germany and Switzerland. He founded the Merovingean dynasty of Frankish rulers, named after Merovic, the legendary ancestor of the Frankish horde.[4] In 496 AD, Clovis adopted the Roman version of Christianity after a battlefield victory, fulfilling a vow to his wife, Clotilda. But like most patchwork governments based on the strength of a single great leader, the Frankish Empire fragmented after his death.

In 567 AD, France was split into three kingdoms. The grandsons of Clovis were each made a king, but the dukes and other nobles wielded more power than their monarchs.[5] By the time Columbanus set foot in France in 591 AD, murder and subtle intrigues had merged the eastern kingdoms of Austrasia and Burgundy under one crown worn by Childebert.[6] His cousin Chlotar ruled the western kingdom of Neustria along the Atlantic coast.

Although Columbanus' ship first landed in Neustria, he refused an invitation to settle in Chlotar's court for unknown reasons. Instead he proceeded on foot with his band of monks to Burgundy, to the lands governed by Childebert. And as he trudged across France, he must have noticed how the rustic farmers clung to their pagan beliefs despite the outward forms of Christianity practised by the nobles. The Frankish priests and bishops seemed to care little for their followers of common blood, concentrating their attentions on the wealthy aristocrats who could shower them with land and gold. According to the Roman Christian historian, Gregory of Tours, the Frankish clergy had largely abandoned Arianism for the Roman version of Christianity. Yet they remained corrupt, openly engaging in murder, theft, and sexual excess.[7] It must have appeared to Columbanus that the Franks were Christian for political purposes only, to gain wealth from abroad or alliances in time of war. For a wandering Celt, their Christian faith must have been a mockery, a religious wasteland devoid of spirituality.

When Columbanus arrived at Childebert's court in Burgundy, he received another surprise. Instead of the sumptuous stronghold he had expected of a Merovingean king, he found only poverty and parsimony. Childebert was poor in gold, lacking the funds to properly administer his government. The scientific methods of agronomy practised by the Celts were unknown in the area and the royal farms produced little surplus. The king was reduced to paying his troops and retainers with parcels of land, diminishing his holdings and his revenues.[8] But the rudest shock of all for Columbanus was Queen Brunhilde, Childebert's mother. Beautiful and ill-tempered, she dominated the kingdom with her strength of personality.

Objective accounts portray Brunhilde as a vicious and vindictive woman who used poison, torture, and the garrote to achieve power.[9] She was a princess of Visigoth Spain, married off to Sigebert of Burgundy to cement an alliance between her father and the Frankish king. At the same time, Brunhilde's sister, Galswintha, was married to Chlotar of Neustria. Galswintha was found strangled shortly after her wedding and the Neustrians strongly suspected that Brunhilde gave the order. Over the years, this festering suspicion caused a great deal of friction between Neustria and Burgundy. When Sigebert mysteriously died from poison in 576 AD, Brunhilde became Queen Regent of Burgundy and Austrasia. Even after her son, Childebert, came of age and assumed the crown, she remained a sinister power behind the throne, guiding his every move.[10]

Childebert was greatly impressed with Columbanus and he begged his mother to let the roving preacher stay in his realm. He may have recognized in these foreign monks a source of knowledge and education that would make his kingdom wealthy and strong. Brunhilde yielded to her son's wishes, perhaps because Columbanus had refused to reside with her rivals in Neustria, perhaps because she saw no threat to her rule from the bedraggled monks. She granted Columbanus a remote plot of land to found his monastery.

In the Vosages hills of Alsace near modern Annegray, Columbanus settled with his twelve disciples. For his monastery,
he chose to rebuild the ruins of a Roman temple to Diana,
possibly because of the local historic veneration of the site.[11] At
first, the distant outposts of Celtic Christianity showed little
prospect for survival. Surrounded by a dark and brooding
forest, the monks laboured day and night to clear the land. The
soil was barren and the first summer's crop was meagre. But
the monks' patient husbandry eventually produced results.
After a few years, they were cultivating large fields and raising
herds of animals. And soon they gained fame among the
Franks for their innovative agricultural methods.

The local tribe surrounding the monastic community of
Annegray were known as Suevians. Impoverished and barbaric even by primitive Frankish standards, the pagan Suevians were soon astonished by the apparently peaceful way of life
of the monks that created such splendid material rewards.
They adopted Christianity and soon Columbanus was besieged
by young men who wanted to join his flock.[12]

The growing number of new recruits in Columbanus' monastery eventually forced him to found two other estab-
lishments at Luxeuil and Fontaine. And in all of the
communities, the religious rule of behaviour followed by the
monks was very strict. Columbanus instituted continuous worship, requiring his monks to chant prayers in relays around the
clock. Silence was enforced when speech was not necessary for
prayer or work. Fasting was common and the normal diet
sparse.[13]

The objective of Columbanus' rule was to overcome the basic
human nature of the monks through rigid training. If successfully followed, the rule theoretically enabled a monk to become
the model Christian, a living representation of the perfection
awaiting the faithful after death. But sexuality was a very real
and constant threat. It was not enough that a monk remain
bodily chaste. He had to be mentally chaste as well, denying
and suppressing every fleeting sexual thought. Since only the
individual monk himself could know his innermost thoughts,
Columbanus recommended frequent introspection to boldly

confront the sin of secret sexual fantasy. If the monk was successful in his internal quest and discovered hidden sexual thoughts, self-inflicted pain and privation were his rewards.

According to legend, Columbanus provided an explicit list of severe penances for even the most trivial of offences. This catalogue became known as the Penitential of Columbanus. But if followed strictly, few monks would have been hardy enough to long endure the discipline. Even the most minor of infractions against the rule was punished with scourging.[14] After the death of Columbanus, many monasteries of Central Europe and Italy embraced his harsh code of Christian crime and punishment until it was eventually superseded by the milder Benedictine Rule. Yet it is likely that the Penitential of Columbanus was largely a creation of Columbanus' successors, made rigid and inflexible by fanatic monks who wanted to outdo their founder with extravagant devotion to the external signs of piety.[15]

After his monasteries were established and prospering, Columbanus turned his attention towards the conversion of those Franks who remained largely pagan. He engaged in extensive missionary work, bringing the Celtic version of Christianity to the farmers and herdsmen overlooked by the wealthy priests who owed allegiance to the Bishop of Rome. But this rapidly earned him the enmity of the Frankish clergy who feared that their decadent lifestyle might be threatened by a purist Christian movement emphasizing poverty and simplicity.

In 602 AD, the Roman Christian bishops of Burgundy and Austrasia demanded that Columbanus appear before them to explain the deviant behaviour of his congregation. Foremost among their grievances was Columbanus' refusal to acknowledge the authority of any bishop of his community. In Celtic practice, the abbot was entirely autonomous, answerable to no higher earthly master. For the Frankish bishops who were as wealthy and powerful as minor nobles, Columbanus was a focus of dissent, an unpredictable force threatening the ecclesiastical power structure.[16] The Frankish bishops were also troubled by the Celtic practice of private confession which kept secret the religious crimes of lay men and women. Public confession placed a great deal of power in the hands of the Roman Christian clergy who could coerce both nobles and commoners with the threat of exposure before an assembled congregation. As a final complaint, the Frankish bishops took exception to the Celtic manner of calculating the date of Easter.[17] The ongoing struggle between the Roman and Celtic branches of Christianity over Easter had little substantive importance. But it did act as a symbol for the claims of supremacy over all Christians made by the Bishop of Rome.

Wisely, Columbanus ignored the summons of the Frankish bishops. But he continued to aggravate his enemies by constantly hurling verbal attacks on them and their way of life. On the issue of Easter, he wrote a letter to Gregory I who was Bishop of Rome at the time. He outlined the history behind the Celtic computation of the date which allowed the celebration to fall on any day of the week instead of limiting it to a Sunday. He also expressed loyalty to the Bishop of Rome as the successor of the Apostle Peter, but he went on to deny the authority of any outsider to interfere with traditional Celtic practices.[18]

If Gregory chose to answer this letter, no record survived. But the words of Columbanus suggesting acceptance of the ecclesiastical supremacy of the Bishop of Rome surfaced in later years to bolster Roman attacks on the Celtic version of Christianity.[19] Taken out of context, it appeared as if Columbanus acknowledged Gregory as the head of the Christian Church with the right to dictate dogma and ritual to the Celts.

As Columbanus grew older, he became a fire and brimstone preacher stalking the countryside. No person was beyond his verbal attacks, no position too high for him to assault. In 610 AD, the Frankish Bishops convened the Synod of Chalon sur Saone to again question the activities of Columbanus. But the result was only a guarded condemnation which had little impact on Columbanus. Only when he earned the hatred of the Queen Regent, Brunhilde, did his preaching career in Burgundy come to an abrupt halt.

Childebert had died in 595 AD, perhaps naturally, perhaps by intrigue. His sons inherited his kingdom with Austrasia going to Theodebert II and Burgundy to Theodoric II. Theodoric was sexually promiscuous and enjoyed a number of casual lovers.[20] This behaviour strongly offended the sexually restrictive views of Columbanus. He publicly chastised the new king at every possible occasion. Eventually, Theodoric relented and took Ermenburga for his wife, the daughter of yet another Spanish Visigoth ruler.

While Columbanus focused on the sleeping arrangements of his king, Brunhilde was living in Austrasia with her other grandson, Theodebert. But he soon tired of her dangerous intrigues. Possibly from fears for his own life, he sent her to Burgundy to live with his brother.

From the moment Brunhilde arrived in the Burgundian court of Theodoric, she was appalled by the influence Columbanus had gained over her grandson. She believed that no priest had the authority to tell a king how to live and whom to sleep with. And for Brunhilde, Ermenburga personified the impertinence of the wild eyed monk who challenged the royal power of the Merovingeans. After several abortive attempts on Ermenburga's life, she convinced Theodoric to banish his wife so he could resume his sexual escapades with his mistresses. And to discredit Columbanus, she encouraged Theodoric to ask the abbot to publicly bless his bastard sons.

Columbanus refused to bless the children and Brunhilde's clever trap sprang shut. If Columbanus had remained true to his Celtic heritage, he would have squirmed free. For a Celt, the circumstances of a person's origin did not reflect on an individual's worth. The entire concept of legitimacy was largely irrelevant in Celtic culture which sanctioned multiple partner marriages. Many of the recognized saints of the Celtic Church were conceived in sexual liaisons that a Roman Christian would have found scandalous. But somewhere during his intellectual and physical travels, Columbanus abandoned the traditional sexual viewpoints of his people, fully embracing the sexual morality of the Roman Christians.

While Roman Christian dogma did not directly condemn an illegitimate child, it did emphasize the sinful nature of the union between the child's mother and father. The property and marriage laws of the Roman Emperors did not recognize the

rights of a child born out of wedlock.[21] As inheritors of the
paradigms of the Empire, the Roman Christians continued to
sort children based on the legal legitimacy of their parents'
relationship. The logic of Augustine contributed toward the
discrimination against the baseborn by allowing the sin at the
time of conception to be passed on as a burden to the offspring
just as the sin of Adam and Eve was passed on to all humanity.

When Columbanus refused to bless the children of Theodoric, he demonstrated that his vision of Christianity was no
longer purely Celtic. But neither was it fully Roman. He behaved as a hybrid Christian, fusing ideas common to both
Ireland and France. On the matters of monastic autonomy,
private confession and Easter, he remained thoroughly Celtic.
But his sexual concepts agreed with the Roman model.

Unable to accept such public humiliation, Theodoric de-
ported Columbanus. He also decreed that all Celtic monks
must accompany him, leaving the dissident monasteries completely in the hands of the Franks. A military escort accompanied Columbanus and his Celtic followers to Nantes where
they were placed on a ship sailing for Ireland. But foul weather
forced the vessel to turn back and it landed in Neustria. Of this
western Frankish kingdom, Chlotar was still ruler. And he had
no love for Brunhilde or her grandchildren, still smarting from
the mysterious loss of his wife so many years earlier.[22] Possibly
to further annoy his Burgundian enemies, he welcomed Columbanus and invited him to settle in Neustria.

But Columbanus refused Chlotar's offer. Instead he ac-
cepted an invitation from Theodebert to live in Austrasia.
Together with his monks, Columbanus rowed down the Rhine
until he reached a part of Austrasia which extended into
Switzerland. Proceeding on foot, he continued until he came to
Breganz where he decided to remain.

A short time later, war broke out between the royal brothers,
Theodoric and Theodebert. At the battle of Tolbiac, Theodoric's
Burgundians defeated Theodebert's Austrasians. Not content
with military victory, Brunhilde arranged the assassination of
her grandson Theodebert, perhaps to repay insulting her with
banishment. Then Burgundy annexed Austrasia. And quite

A female dancing figure, 3rd Century AD, from Gaul.

A Gallo-Roman representation of motherhood. Detail from a delicate relief of the 'Three Mothers' from the town of Vertillum, in Burgundy.

The sheela-na-gig from Kilpeck, Herefordshire; the representation of a fertility goddess incorporated into Christianity.

St Brigid (Brigid goddess and Brigit saint are fused these days). Brigid was the goddess of fertility and love.

Queen Maev (Meabh), the archetypal
Celtic sensual woman.

Cuchulain represents a potent lover as well as
a warrior in Celtic mythology.

The Curse of Macha – Macha symbolises Celtic
sexuality in Irish mythology. Pregnant, she is
forced to run a race against the king's horses. She
begs to be allowed to have her children first. The
king denies her and she races, wins the race, gives
birth at the moment of winning and then curses
Ulster – that the men of Ulster will suffer every
seven years from the birth pangs.

Powerful sexual themes
permeate Celtic mytho-
logy, such as the women
who dwelt undersea who
tried to persuade the
hero Brian to stay with
them.

The children of Lir are the archetypal victims of sexual jealousy.

Epona, the horse goddess, is one of the many goddesses represented in Celtic mythology.

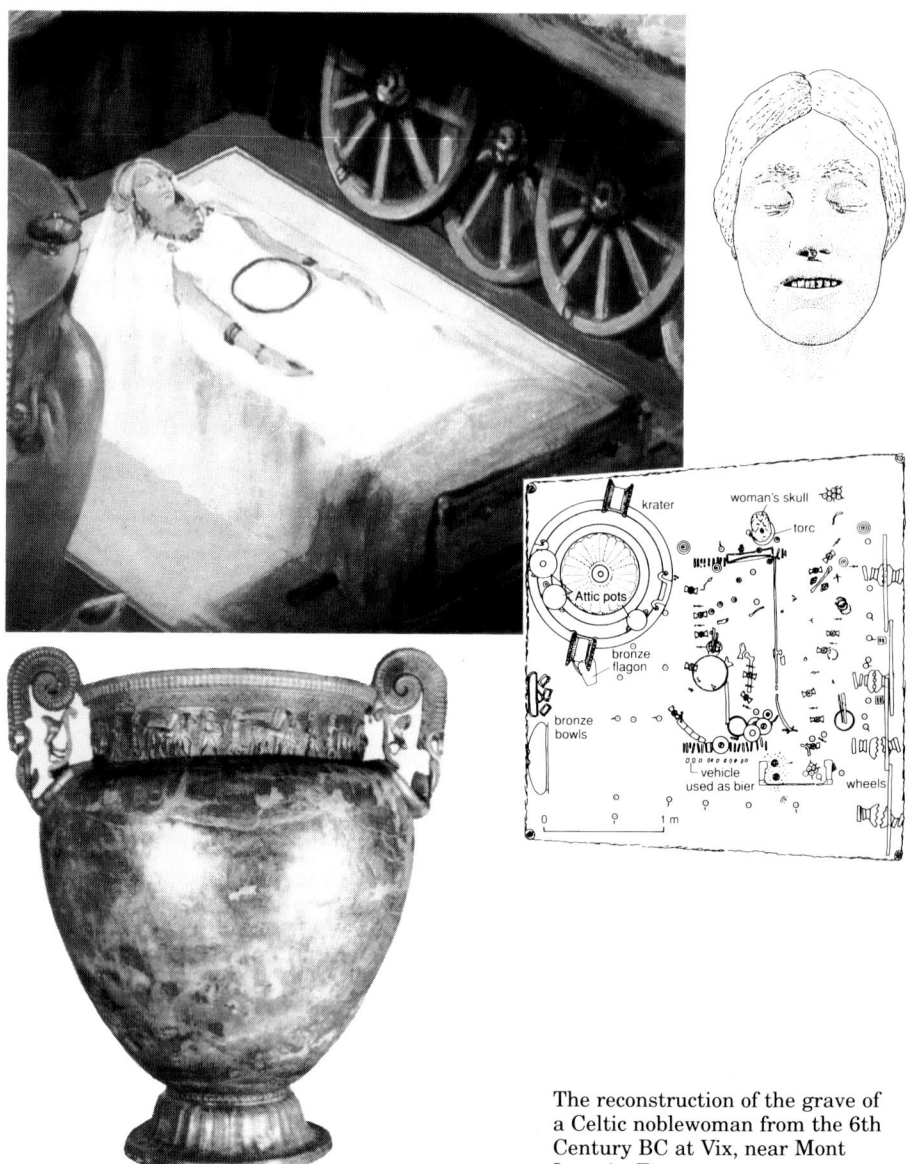

The reconstruction of the grave of a Celtic noblewoman from the 6th Century BC at Vix, near Mont Lassois, France.

Boudica and her daughters. Boudica, ruler of the Iceni, was
publicly flogged and her daughters raped, which resulted in
her raising the tribes of southern Britain against the
Romans in AD 60. Boudica is considered a powerful symbol
of Celtic womanhood.

Queen Guinevere (Gwenhwyvar in Celtic) by William Morris. She became the wife of Arthur but her infidelity with Lancelot led to the fall of Arthur.

suddenly, Columbanus found himself once more in the lands controlled by his bitter enemies, Brunhilde and Theodoric.

When he heard the news of Tolbiac, Columbanus prepared to flee to Italy, to the lands beyond Frankish control. But one of his followers was ill, a monk named Gall who had been with Columbanus for years. Despite Gall's infirmity, Columbanus insisted that he trudge with the others over the high mountain ranges of the Alps. But Gall refused and the two men exchanged angry words. Hurling a curse at his former companion, Columbanus left for Italy. Gall eventually recovered and remained in Switzerland to found the monastery of St. Gall which would gain prominence in the centuries to come.[23]

Columbanus continued south into Lombardy. At Bobbio he halted, establishing yet another monastic centre. This time he chose the ruins of a Christian church for his site. And there he died in 615 AD.

For his legacy, Columbanus left behind a number of devotional poems and letters which partly reveal his vision of Christianity. In addition, the educational tradition he established in his many monasteries persisted through the centuries. The preservation of classical learning undertaken by his monks helped to fuel the Carolingean Renaissance.

Three years after the death of Columbanus, a monk named Jonas entered the community of Bobbio. He interviewed many of the men who had lived and wandered with Columbanus. Eventually he wrote the *Life of Columbanus*. Throughout the biography, Jonas portrayed the abbot as a man tormented by sexual desire. He recounted a tale from the youth of Columbanus, of a time when the leader of monks was under the care of an elderly woman hermit. The old Celtic hag constantly spoke of the wiles of Eve, Delilah, and all the evil women of Christian myth who deceived men. Impressed by this incessant lecturing, Columbanus decided to forsake all females.[24] But the decision of his intellect could not fully control the desires of his body.

Perhaps an element of envy lay in the steadfast refusal of Columbanus to bless the children of Theodoric. According to Jonas of Bobbio, Columbanus' decision to give up women and embrace monastic chastity had cost him many a sleepless night as he grappled with his suppressed sexuality. And it is possible that the thought of Theodoric enjoying the pleasures of multiple lovers angered him enough to risk the destruction of all he had built.

*

At the beginning of the seventh century AD, Columbanus found himself in a unique religious position. As an autocratic Celtic abbot independent of any formal religious hierarchy, he could pick and choose the Christian dogma that suited him. In his external ritual, he appeared to remain thoroughly Celtic. But for his sexual paradigms, he aligned himself with the Roman Christians. He was a hybrid Christian, a clergyman who was neither Celtic nor Roman.

Within the Christian communities, it was common practice to monitor the behaviour of others to discover deviance from the rules of conduct. If a sexual sinner was exposed, the priority of punishment was admonition, penance, and expulsion from the community, depending on the magnitude of the offenoe.[25] When Columbanus tried to impose his vision of Christian sexual behaviour on a king, he exemplified the growing influence of Roman Christian sexual paradigms among the Celts. In the past, the monks of Ireland and Britain like Columcille were more concerned with their own behaviour than with the behaviour of others. Shut up within the walls of their monasteries, they focused on their own private salvation. But Columbanus took his sexual ethic beyond the cloister, demanding that all people bring their intimate relationships into conformity with his sexual beliefs.

Columbanus was unwise to pursue such a policy in Burgundy. The society may have been barbaric by Roman and Celtic standards, but it was stable. No forces threatened total annihilation either internally or externally, and the Franks were unwilling to change their sexual paradigms to please the whims of a foreign monk. For tampering with such a fundamental issue as sexuality, Columbanus was lucky to have received deportation instead of death.

Columbanus' attempt to dictate the sexual practices of a king also crossed a political boundary between religion and state. If Brunhilde had not convinced Theodoric to defy Columbanus, the abbot would have retained a degree of control over the activities of the king. Columbanus' influence could easily have spilled out of the bed chamber and into the political arena of the throne room. The Franks were not yet willing to share civil power with any religious authority.

But Columbanus worked in strange lands inhabited by men and women who did not share his cultural paradigms. In his home islands to the north, the influence of abbots was spreading beyond the confines of their monasteries, touching the sexual behaviour of both pagans and Christians. Gradually, the farmer in the field and the king in the hillfort were forced to confront the celibate monk who wanted to decree how all people should express their sexuality.

10

The Cult of The Virgin Mary

Establishing control over the sexual habits of their followers was a formidable task for the Christian clergy. Behind closed doors, a lover's delight in the body of another was a secret matter, revealed to a priest only through careless gossip or the ritual of confession. Even the ascetics sworn to celibacy occasionally strayed from the rule of chastity when opportunity arose, unable to suppress the demands of their flesh. In the heat of passion, many of the Christian regulations were ignored.

To help channel the normal sexual inclinations of their congregation, the early Christian theologians introduced love for an ideal as a substitute for love between two people. They believed that an abstract concept was a more satisfying focus for love, since an ideal was constant, never disappointing human devotion and ardour. A mortal man or woman could be unfaithful, capable of betrayal and deception. But an ideal was permanent, unchanging and immutable. And if the ideal was personified, if it was given a fair face and form, the demand for sexual abstinence from its human lover was a burden easier to bear.

At first, the early Christians concentrated their ideal love on Jesus and the pure spirituality of the godhead represented by the Father. Because of the patriarchal paradigms inherited by the Christians from both Rome and Judea, the triple aspects of their god were traditionally portrayed as a male father and son linked by a genderless spirit. For heterosexual men, the concept of replacing earthly love for a woman with spiritual love for a remote male deity may have been difficult to accept.

In addition, the Christian God depicted in the Old Testament was often harsh and autocratic, more like an aloof monarch than a soothing lover. To provide a female principle as a complement to the male love ideal, the early Christians elevated the status of Mary, the human mother of Jesus.[1]

For the first four hundred years after the death of Jesus, the position of Mary in Christian theology was somewhat unsettled. Scripture claimed that she was impregnated without sexual intercourse by the Holy Spirit, an aspect of the Christian God lacking specific gender. She was a virgin at the time, presumably living in a celibate marriage with her husband, Joseph. But if the same scriptures were read carefully, they suggested that Mary was the mother of many children, not only Jesus.[2] This seemed to indicate that Mary was a sexual being at some time in her life, a woman who was both lover and mother.

But as the male celibates gained power within the Christian movement, they quickly squelched the defenders of sexuality and marriage who cited scripture for support. The Christian male clergy who called themselves virgins had to divest Mary of her sexuality in order to make her a love ideal worthy of their adoration. The early Christian theologians invented a fictitious earlier marriage for Joseph, claiming that Mary was the stepmother of Joseph's children. It did not trouble them that their own scriptures made no mention of any previous wife for Joseph. But even this granted a degree of legitimacy to marriage, a state the celibates claimed was inferior to their own chastity. They found it necessary to also impute virginity to Joseph. So they discarded their first fanciful explanation for the siblings of Jesus and transformed them into cousins.[3] Now the celibate theologians could be content, certain that the mortal parents of their god were not tainted by any trace of normal human sexuality in their marriage.

But stripping Mary of her sexuality was not enough to make her into a perfect female love ideal. The male celibates who controlled Roman Christian doctrine had to remove all connection between Mary and other women. If they failed to do so, love for the feminine ideal represented by Mary could easily transfer to a living, breathing female. So they violated the concept of childbirth, taking from Mary another natural process she shared with other women.

Near the end of the second century AD, a forged gospel attributed to James, the brother of Jesus, received wide circulation. Roman Christians eventually rejected the writings, although they were accepted by the Eastern Christian Church. However the part of the Gospel of James supporting the doctrine of virgin childbirth crept into Roman Christian dogma to bolster the dehumanization of Mary.

In an almost pornographic passage, James recounted the examination of Mary's hymen after the birth of Jesus by the midwife, Salome. As if she were inspecting the quality of meat, Salome plunged her hand into Mary's vagina until she encountered the obstruction signifying that Mary remained a virgin. For her impertinence, Salome's hand was severely burned. Only when she held the infant Jesus was her flesh miraculously restored.[4]

James also mentioned that Mary gave birth without pain. According to the Roman Christian doctrine of original sin, the suffering of childbirth was the punishment levied on all women for the sin of Eve. Augustine of Hippo was quick to fuse this idea with his own teachings, claiming that Mary gave birth without pain because she conceived without carnal pleasure. By denying the natural suffering associated with birth, another connection between Mary and other women was severed.

Although it was not mentioned in the Gospel of James, the Roman Christians added a further refinement to their doctrine of virgin childbirth. After the delivery of Jesus, there was no afterbirth. In Latin, the Roman Christian theologians used the word *sordes* to describe afterbirth, a term which translates as filth. For the celibate the process of childbirth was conceived in corruption and resulted in corruption. Only Mary was spared the sordid circumstances common to all other women.

On the surface, the alteration of Mary's normal birth process was designed to show that she was pure and perfect. But it had the additional effect of dehumanizing women as a group since they could never attain the ideal represented by Mary.

She alone was non-sexual, an almost genderless vessel to incubate the Christian man-god. All other women were impure and imperfect. For the celibate men who eventually came to dominate Western Christianity, Mary was the only female worthy of respect.

The gradual transformation of Mary from sexual mother into feminine ideal took many centuries. In 432 AD, the Council of Ephesus made her officially the Mother of God, permanently separating her from all other women in Christian doctrine. In the later Middle Ages, orders of monks and nuns were established to devote themselves to the worship of the female principle represented by Mary. The Christians eventually created Mariology, a branch of theology exclusively concerned with the mystical nature of Mary. And generally, the greatest veneration to Mary was displayed by Christian men, not Christian women.

In part, the presence of a woman in the male Christian cosmology was necessary to address the problem posed by pagan worship of a mother goddess. As the Christians spread through Western Europe, they had difficulty eradicating secret devotion to the female fertility principle personified as a goddess with various names. The quasi-deification of Mary provided a partial solution to the problem, allowing pagans to transfer their veneration of a local goddess to a Christian demi-goddess. Sergius, a Bishop of Rome in the late seventh century AD, sanctioned this concept by mandating that the Christian feast days dedicated to Mary take place on dates previously associated with pagan goddesses.[5]

Many of the later medieval statues of Mary showed her crushing a snake beneath her foot. In Christian and Hebrew myth, the serpent was a representation of the male devil who tempted Eve in the Garden of Eden. But the pagan meaning of the snake symbol was neither male nor evil. It was an aspect of the Mother Goddess, a beast who exemplified rebirth when it shed its old skin during the growth process.[6] By stepping on the snake, Mary demonstrated her victory over the competing female principles found in pagan beliefs.

*

For the Celtic druid, the essence of the universe was female. All life, all creation was a manifestation of the goddess. Danu was the fertile Mother, representing the cycle of birth, death, and rebirth. Integral to the Celtic view of the world were the goddesses Brigid, the Mórrígán, and Macha, each with triple aspects personifying a wide range of feminine attributes.

When the Christians introduced the story of Mary into the Celtic lands, the converted druids immediately understood her as a fertility principle analogous to the goddesses of their own culture. They transferred much of the symbolic meaning associated with the Celtic goddesses onto Mary. But to make her fit more closely into their world view, they initially had to ignore the Roman Christian distortions to sexuality and childbirth which made her remote from other women. They emphasized the concept of Mary as eternal mother, encouraging men and women to turn to her for spiritual refuge in times of trouble.

With a unique cultural chauvinism, the Celts also adopted Mary as one of their own, weaving fanciful tales linking her with Celtic heritage. They made Brigid of Kildare into Mary's companion, the foster mother of Jesus in accordance with the Celtic tradition of fosterage. Despite the fact that St. Ita lived five centuries after Mary, she was portrayed fondling the infant Jesus on her lap to give Mary a moment's respite from the task of motherhood. Columcille claimed that Mary appeared to him regularly at Iona. And the Celts alleged that Mary's legendary parents, Anne and Joachim, were Irish by birth and later immigrated to Israel.

To demonstrate the special position accorded to Mary in Celtic society, the Irish created a distinctive spelling of her name. Máire was the common form of Mary. But the virgin mother of the Christian God was termed Muire. And in accordance with the Celtic custom of tracing ancestry through the mother, Jesus was often identified in literature only as mac Mhuire, the son of Mary.[7]

By the middle of the eighth century AD, the Celtic version of the cult of Mary was widespread. Her followers venerated relics of dubious authenticity, including a lock of her hair and a tattered remnant of a garment she made for Jesus. Poets chanted her praises, demonstrating the intense intimacy they felt with her. Blathmac called her kinswoman and accused the Jews of the heinous crime of *fingal*, or kin slaying.[8] Pilib Bocht ó hUiginn named her 'The Master Stroke of Women', a term borrowed from the game of hurley calculated to ingratiate her with sportsmen. And Angus the Culdee spoke at length of Mary's sexuality and the mystery which enabled a virgin to give birth.

But in their worship of Mary, many Celtic Christians trod a fine line between heresy and orthodoxy. Much to the consternation of the Roman Christians, many of the Celts continued to look at Mary as a fertility principle, as an avatar of the native goddesses. In their literature and prayers, the Celts had little difficulty speaking directly of Mary's breasts and womb, the external organs defining her as female. Yet they used clever and ambiguous words, making enigmatic statements which could be interpreted by Roman Christians either as deviation or as orthodoxy. In legend, Columcille's birth was preceded by an angelic annunciation and the mother of Senán was spared the pains of childbirth, symbolically linking both women to Mary. But when Celtic writers were questioned about the potential heresy of their statements about Mary, they used their ambiguity as a shield.[9]

The early Celtic portrayal of Mary was less mystical, less ethereal than the vision adopted by the Roman Christians. But the earthy image of Mary offered by the Celtic poets and storytellers was unsuitable for the celibate men who struggled with their repressed sexuality in their monastic cells. The monks countered with their own artistic vision of Mary found in a portrait of *The Book of Kells*. Her eyes were unnaturally large with high arched brows. The child she held looked more like a wizened old man than an infant. The entire composition suggested an austere woman of Byzantine origin, a female from a land as distant and remote from Kells as heaven itself.[10]

To insure that Mary was worthy of their adoration, the celibate monks had to refashion her into a creature of the Otherworld who knew no passion, who suffered no pain. During the tenth century AD, a story circulated claiming that Jesus was born from Mary's skull instead of her vagina, analogous to the parthenogenesis of Athena from the head of Zeus. This was an attempt to strip the process of natural childbirth from Mary using a fiction not supported by Christian scripture. After the Anglo-Norman invasion of Ireland a few centuries later, some Celtic ascetics challenged Mary's sexuality by alleging that she was impregnated through her ear and not through her vagina.[11] Although neither of these novel ideas describing Mary's birth process received wide acceptance, they demonstrated the gradual metamorphosis of the Celtic image of Mary as she changed from fertile earth mother into sexless virgin. When the Roman Christians eventually achieved ecclesiastical dominance over Celtic lands, they tolerated no further deviations from their official doctrines regarding Mary.

When Mary was completely shorn of her links with human women, the Celtic ascetics used her as a wedge to separate the genders. For men, she represented a sexually untouchable ideal, a mother image who shamed them for lustful thoughts and deeds. For women, she was an image of frigidity, a female who had perfectly repressed her sexuality. Priests no longer had to police the bedrooms of their followers. Whenever Christian men and women engaged in their duty of procreation, the image of Mary crept between them to deny pleasure.

Brigid of Kildare

As the followers of the cult of Mary struggled to impose their ideal of female perfection on the Celtic people, they discovered that the pagan goddesses were not their only rivals. A woman named Brigid had gained such prominence among the Christian Celts that many revered her more highly than the official mother of God. Her supporters even dubbed her the 'Mary of the Gael', a title emphasizing Brigid's competition with Mary.

Brigid was not mentioned in the contemporary historical sources of her time and she may not have existed beyond the imagination of later writers and mythmakers. But she had the same impact on succeeding generations as if she had been a living and breathing woman. According to Cogitus, her first biographer, she was born in 455 AD at Faughart in County Down.[1] Her name meant brightness and was probably derived from the Celtic sun deity Brigantia.[2] She lived in a time when Christianity was new in Celtic lands, in a time when literacy was a rare achievement. Virtually all of the chronicles of the period were composed more than a century after Brigid's birth, compiled from legends and oral testimony. The concept of Brigid the saint was probably superimposed on the goddess Brigid of the Tuatha Dé Danaan. This gave a Christian focus to a druid religious tradition, fusing the old religion with the new. It also granted Christian patronage to the triple attributes of healing, fertility, and ironwork represented by the old goddess.[3]

Brigid was the daughter of the druid Dubhtach and a female bondservant of low status named Broicsech. In his writings, Julius Caesar claimed that the societal position of Celtic and

Roman slaves were similar in all respects.[4] But the Celtic mythological cycles and the Brehon Law depict a much milder form of slavery. Broicsech was probably required to work at a menial task without the freedom to come and go as she pleased. But she did not live or die at the whim of her master, and like any Celtic female, she had the right to refuse unwanted sexual advances. The societal niche of bondservant was usually filled by debtors and prisoners captured in war.[5]

In common with other Celtic saints, many fantastic events surrounded Brigid's birth and childhood. She was born on *Bealtaine*, on the first of May. It was a mystical day for the Celts, commemorating the changing of seasons and the arrival of the Tuatha Dé Danaan in Ireland. Like the cold fire burning in the breast of Danu, flames that did not scorch leaped from the infant Brigid's head. At some point, she adopted Christianity, perhaps from her mother, perhaps from the preaching of another.[6] When she was grown, she went to pray at the chapel of Bishop Ibhair. The night before, he had dreamed that the Virgin Mary would appear before his congregation the following day. And as his followers waited anxiously for the miracle, Brigid walked into their church. To save his reputation as a prophet, Ibhair claimed that Brigid was the Mary he had envisioned. Afterwards, she was called the 'Mary of the Gael'.[7]

As a young woman, Brigid annoyed Dubhtach by giving away vast quantities of his goods to the needy. Although the Celts followed the charitable custom of *poltach* to support the poor, Brigid carried almsgiving to an extreme, even donating her father's sword to a beggar. To removed this blight from his finances, Dubhtach decided to place Brigid as a bondservant in the kitchens of the King of Leinster. The king refused to accept her, claiming to be impressed by Brigid's piety.[8] But perhaps he was merely trying to preserve his wealth and did not want to be troubled by a bondservant who gave away her master's goods.

A short time later, a suitor appeared asking Dubhtach for Brigid's hand in marriage. But Brigid wanted to remain chaste. To discourage the eager young man, she thrust her finger into her eye, pulling it from the socket until it dangled on her cheek. Appalled by Brigid's self-mutilation, the suitor's romantic arduor quickly vanished.[9]

Celtic women did not shy from extreme measures to avoid a demanding suitor. Long before Brigid plucked out her eye, the story of the Exile of the Sons of Uisliu became part of Celtic myth. Conchobhar, the King of Ulster, sought the hand of Derdriu. But she loved Noísiu and together they ran off to a foreign land. Eventually Conchobhar's guarantee of safety lured them back to Ulster. When they were in Conchobar's territory, he ordered his warriors to kill Noísiu and capture Derdriu. But at her first opportunity, Derdriu dashed her head against a boulder, choosing suicide over a passionless marriage with the man who had murdered her lover.[10] Her act of self-destruction was not an indictment of marriage or sexuality, but a response to the abuse of power by a treacherous monarch. By preferring death to Conchobhar's bed. Derdriu heaped enduring shame upon him.

But there was no indication that Brigid's suitor was a demanding villain. The sexual relationship implicit in marriage was her primary concern, not the kindness or honour of her suitor. Her self-mutilation to escape marriage was uncalled for by the circumstances, an innovative and surprising act not grounded in the paradigms of Celtic society. In one stroke, Brigid cleverly complied with the Christian teachings to avoid both sex and suicide. Casting aside the Celtic sexual viewpoints, she dramatically emphasized her desire for Christian chastity, her need to shun all intimate contact with the opposite sex. But Brigid was largely the creation of Christian male celibates who controlled access to literacy in the Celtic lands. She reflected their values and their views of the feminine ideal. As with Mary, they moulded Brigid into a model for how Christian women should act, not how they did act. And a portrait emerged of a woman who believed that marriage was a horror worse than disfigurement and blindness.

After her narrow escape from the conjugal bed, Brigid decided to found a monastery of her own, a place of refuge from the threat of male sexuality. She chose for her site Kildare, known as *cill daire* in Old Irish which translates as the church of the oaks. In druid times, the grove of Kildare may have been sacred, a place made holy by centuries of religious ceremony.[11] To define the boundaries of her domain, she spread her cloak upon the ground and built a sanctuary which no man could enter.

Christian women soon gathered to emulate Brigid and to vow permanent virginity. A community of women who shunned all contact with men was a novel concept for insular Celtic culture. Their myths made no direct mention of the necessity of lifelong female virginity for religious ritual. In an agricultural society valuing fertility, childbirth was important to the continuity of the community. But some evidence has survived indicating that a temporary condition of virginity was necessary for certain sacred practices. A society of women later called 'nuns' by the Christian chroniclers served the needs of the ancient High King at Tara. When a new king was crowned, he publicly mated with one of these women as a proxy for the promiscuous goddess Maev. If indeed the 'nun' was a virgin, it was a transitory state in preparation for ceremonial inter- course.[12] Another indirect reference to virginity appeared in a fragmentary poem describing the naming of Lough Erne. This work mentioned maidens who were the priestesses of Maev, but again did not emphasize the permanence of their virginity.

In early Roman myth, the term *virgines* did not refer to the level of a woman's sexual experience with men. Instead it was used to describe a woman who lived independently from male society. Celtic myth also depicted women who did not depend on men. Scáthach and Aife were both proficient warriors and effective leaders who lived apart from male society. But these women were fiercely sexual, making love frequently and pas- sionately. It was possible that Brigid and her virgins were a Christianized version of this traditional Celtic motif.

Although they professed to be Christians, the virgins of Kildare were not fully analogous to the orders of celibate Christian nuns which began to appear in the fifth century AD. While both the virgins of Kildare and the nuns cloistered themselves to escape any contact with men, nuns remained under the close supervision of the male priesthood. Roman

Christian bishops dictated religious ritual and guarded the sexuality of the nuns with the zeal of harem eunuchs. The labour assigned to nuns was usually menial and ignoble, with little true significance in the rites of the Roman Christian religion.

But the virgins of Kildare answered to no man, Christian or pagan. No king and no bishop controlled their activities. Their primary duty was to maintain an eternal flame, a druid custom that had its roots in the fires associated with the goddesses Brigid and Danu. For seven centuries, they kept the blaze continuously burning until the Roman Christian Archbishop of Dublin ordered it extinguished in 1220 AD, forty years after the Anglo-Norman invasion of Ireland.[13] And this duty empowered them with a sense of the heroic, with a sense of religious purpose not usually available to Christian women.

Their independence from men and their sacred fire linked the virgins of Kildare more closely with the pagan priestesses of Vesta than with Roman Christian nuns. The virgins dedicated to Vesta vowed not to engage in sexual relations with men for a period of thirty years. During this time, they kept alight a sacred flame before a likeness of the goddess. After their term of office expired, they could choose to remain in the service of Vesta or enter into a relationship with a man. But if a holy virgin violated her oath and took a male lover, the other priestesses of Vesta punished her with live burial.

The function of the Vestal Virgins in Roman society was complex. The eternal flame they tended eventually came to represent the health of the Empire. If the flame was extinguished, the Empire would fall. And as guardians of the welfare of Rome, the priestesses of Vesta enjoyed enormous prestige. They were wed to the spirit of Rome and bore the official title of *Amata,* or beloved.[14] They were the embodiment of Roman culture and their virginity symbolized the unbroken unity of that culture.

The virginity of the priestesses of Vesta was not a tacit denunciation of sexuality in general.[15] Their religious function demanded that they abstain from heterosexual activity. Yet in their temple was the Palladium, a fertility object whose exact nature was shrouded in mystery. One Roman tradition held that it was the sceptre of King Priam of Troy shaped like a penis. And since the Palladium was the male principle on which the Empire depended, the Vestal Virgins were also charged with its protection.[16]

In all likelihood, there was no direct connection between the virgins of Kildare and the virgins of Vesta. About a hundred years before Brigid was born, the fires of Vesta were extinguished by order of the Christian Emperors. By the time Brigid founded her enclave, the pagan gods of Rome had lost most of their following. Yet in prehistory, the Celtic and Italic peoples were closely related branches of the Indo-European migrations.[17] They split into separate societies approximately 2000 BC. Perhaps both groups shared a common cultural motif involving the mystery of a sacred fire tended by women. And the requirement of virginity was a later development, the demand of an overbearing patriarchy.

As nominal Christian nuns, the virgins of Kildare shared with their Roman Christian sisters a loathing for sexual relationships with men. But they may not have been completely celibate. Brigid herself shared her bed with Darlughdacha whose name means 'daughter of the sun god Lugh'. On one occasion, Darlughdacha looked lustfully at a passing warrior. To punish and purify her, Brigid made her walk in shoes filled with hot coals. Presumably, Brigid took Darlughdacha back into her bed when the woman had suffered enough for her heterosexual flirtation. And to further insure Darlughdacha's future loyalty, Brigid granted her the right of succession as the next Abbess of Kildare.[18]

The early Christian chronicles and biographies of the saints did not directly address lesbian relationships in Celtic society. These works were created and preserved by celibate scribes who lived and worked in an exclusively male environment. They perceived women only as female caricatures who tempted and deceived, viewing them only in terms of their impact on men. Since they believed that men were inherently more rational than women, they tended to praise females who imitated male behaviour. And they were unconcerned with the bedroom activities of two women who may have made love together.[19] The scribes recorded the story of Brigid and Darlughdacha as a morality tale to demonstrate sin and redemption while ignoring its lesbian implications. As if it had no importance for the Christian sexual ethic, they left intact a description of the relationship between the two women which implied intimacy beyond friendship, beyond teacher and pupil.

Brigid lived and died in a time when Celtic sexual paradigms were in flux, in a time when old ideas were melding with new. Perhaps it was unclear exactly what the vision of Christian sexuality entailed. Perhaps she thought that Christian celibacy meant simply abstaining from sexual contact with men, that frustrating her personal fertility was enough to satisfy the new god. Whatever Brigid believed, she was willing to maim herself to avoid sex with a man while opening her arms to embrace a woman.

To further isolate the community of Kildare from men, Bishop Mel ordained Brigid into the priesthood and made her a bishop.[20] This enabled her to perform the Christian Eucharistic ceremony herself, eliminating the need for a male priest to enter her compound. While the Roman Christians eagerly stripped women of any ecclesiastical function, the Celtic Christians gave them high positions in their church. And after Brigid's death, the Celtic clergy continued to grant the Abbesses of Kildare the same dignity and honours as a male bishop until the Roman Christians ended the practice in the twelfth century AD.[21]

*

For six hundred years, the competition between the Virgin Mary and the virgin Brigid was fierce. Both women represented unrealistic views of female sexuality and the female role in society. Both women were creations of celibate men, idealized visions that diverged greatly from the reality of flesh and bone females. And with their cultural chauvinism, the veneration of the Celts often elevated the native Brigid over the imported Mary. But for the Christians, both Brigid and

Mary served a similar function. They were ideals of perfection designed to break the old habits of female behaviour.

Although the musings of no druid philosopher survived, Celtic sexual morality prior to the arrival of Christianity appeared to be based almost entirely on habit springing from cultural paradigms. A sexual liaison was morally correct if the act fell within the accepted customs of the society. An individual could choose a sexual partner with minimal moral difficulty, with no battle of scruples analysing the right or wrong of the act or the relationship.[22] This non-analytical approach to sexuality was itself a paradigm, a pattern of behaviour ingrained in Celtic people from birth.

Mary represented an opposite approach to sexual morality. She was an ideal, a standard of behaviour created as a guide against which all sexual activity should be measured. Prior to acting on a sexual impulse, the moral criteria embodied by Mary demanded careful reflection and analysis of the intended conduct and its moral implications. Since the ideal of Mary was strongly biased against sexual activity in general, her followers suffered from a paralysis of action. Their bodies prompted them to approach sex while their analytical intellects urged them to abstain.

Lengthy pondering of an ideal prior to action did not appear to be a native Celtic trait. Each man and woman carried with them the paradigms that made action reflexive, not reflective. The analytical mode of behaviour originated in the cultures of the Mediterranean and was imported into Celtic lands by sword and by persuasion. The Roman Christians devoted a considerable amount of intellectual energy to establishing the ideal of Mary and translating it into practice. With their own cultural chauvinism, they characterized the non-analytical approach to morality as primitive and unenlightened, failing to recognize that all action was a blend of habit and reflection.

A pattern of sexual behaviour based on the analysis of an ideal could not be assimilated by the Celts in one generation or even in one century. It was too fundamental, too drastic a change from their old way of thinking. So as a middle ground between pure habit and pure analysis, the Celts created

Brigid. She did not whimsically use sexuality to gain power and pleasure without considering the right or wrong of her acts. Yet she was a woman human enough to recognize her need to hold Darlughdacha close to her in the dark hours of the night. She stood between total sexual abstinence and total sexual indulgence.

When the Roman Christians gained full ecclesiastical control of all the Celtic lands after the Anglo-Norman invasions of Ireland and Scotland, they suppressed the cult of Brigid. Eventually, they even stripped her of her sainthood, demoting her to a folklore figure. Brigid, who was a bishop, who depended on no man, violated the basic world view of the Roman Christian hierarchy. The male celibates felt far less threatened with Mary as the exclusive female ideal, a docile handmaiden who had no ideas or opinions of her own.

During the centuries of the Celtic adjustment to Christian beliefs, the concepts of both Brigid and Mary were instrumental in changing the sexual paradigms of both men and women. Sexuality no longer hinged on habit or custom alone. Christian women were encouraged to carefully reflect on the chastity of the feminine ideal and to use their intellect to suppress any sexual desire they might feel. Christian men would measure all women against the abstract ideal and condemn as harlots any human women who displayed sexual passion. The ultimate result was a people prone to sexual obsession and at war with their own desires.

12

Power and Sexuality

In the moral landscape envisioned by the early Christians, the universe was divided into the domains of good and evil.[1] On one side was the spiritual kingdom ruled by their God, the essence of all that was bright and pure. Opposed to him was the dark and destructive empire of Satan. An eternal battle raged between the two camps for mastery of the universe. By definition, Christianity was godly and all other religions or philosophies were demonic. A further dissection of morality occurred when the individual Christian sects identified themselves with good and assigned their Christian rivals to the realm of evil. In this bi-polar world view, Christians measured all ideas and actions against a doctrinal standard to determine whether they were inspired by their God or his sinister opponent.

For Christians who imagined themselves allied with the forces of good in a great cosmic conflict against evil, power was an essential ingredient for survival. Without spiritual power, Christians believed that they would be helpless to resist the snares and traps devised by demons. The exercise of spiritual power was found in the conquest of the self, in the strength to deny food to a hungry belly or a lover's warmth to a cold and lonely bed. It enabled the Red Martyr to embrace a painful death and the White Martyr to endure a lifetime of foreign exile. When Christians reached the limits of human spiritual power, they often begged for assistance from unseen entities associated with the domain of good. This metaphysical pursuit of control was akin to magic, a striving to use beliefs about the nature of the universe to shape the course of internal and external events.

But some Christian sects saw benefit in exercising direct physical power in the world of mortal men and women. Since they believed that demonic forces actively influenced the negative and destructive events of life, many Christians did not hesitate to wield spear and sword against their enemies of flesh and bone. And their bi-polar logic classified all people who did not believe and practise the same doctrine as nefarious emissaries of Satan.

The concept of evil kept at bay by the exercise of power on behalf of good was a Hebrew paradigm carried into Christianity by the Gospels and the letters of the Apostles.[2] Christ wielded power to cast demons out of people. He granted his followers the same power over 'unclean spirits' which they used to justify casting people out of the Christian community who violated the rules of behaviour and belief.[3] In this dualistic view of the world, power was integral to maintaining the stability of the universe and the doctrinal unity of the various Christian sects.

The words of Christ recorded in the Gospel of Matthew encouraged a confrontational approach to Christian relationships with themselves and with the world around them. Christ claimed he had not come to bring peace on the earth but to set people at odds with one another over matters of faith.[4] Many Christians appeared to accept this proposition by developing a process of moral classification to determine whether an idea, person or action was evil. Whether pagan or rival Christian, adversaries classified as evil had to be overcome with words of persuasion, threats of damnation, or armies of conquest. For most Christians who believed that they held a monopoly on truth and goodness, compromise was unthinkable. The result was a competitive behaviour model in which survival depended on the effective exercise of power to defend a belief system and impose it on others. For the groups who failed to develop adequate paradigms of power, for the Gnostics and Arians and Celts, a Christian-dominated world had little mercy.

Particularly adept at the exercise of temporal power were

the Bishops of Rome. Onto the competitive concepts of Christianity, they grafted many of the imperial paradigms inherited from the Roman Emperors. They firmly believed that Rome was the heart of the civilized world destined to impose an authoritarian ecclesiastical hierarchy on all Christians and pagans. To support their centralized autocratic views, they claimed divine right based on an interpretation of scripture rejected by many of their rival Christian sects.[5] And in accordance with their confrontational bi-polar beliefs, any who disputed their claims were evil.

After the collapse of the Roman Empire, the various Bishops of Rome wielded temporal power with varying degrees of effectiveness depending on their personal abilities. Initially, they concentrated on establishing dominance over other Christian sects and consolidating their financial and social position on the Italian peninsula. In the regions of the eastern Mediterranean, the ambitions of the Bishops of Rome met with little success. Perhaps because of their own stable and well established hierarchies, the Eastern Christians refused to acknowledge Rome as the legitimate seat of Christ's successor on earth. Frustrated, the Bishops of Rome turned their attention westward and northward, toward Spain, France, and beyond the English Channel to Britain.[6]

*

When Gregory I became Bishop of Rome in 590 AD, he immediately reorganized the administration of the vast Italian estates owned by the Roman Christian Church to generate additional revenues. Using the newly created wealth, he began to expand his influence among the kings of France, Spain and northern Italy. He accepted the religious submission of the Lombard king whose Roman Christian wife cleverly used bedroom politics to accomplish his conversion from the Arian sect. In Spain, Gregory's representatives also convinced the king of the Visigoths to abandon Arianism. Both monarchs were amply rewarded financially and politically.[7] Eventually, he financed a missionary expedition to England. In 597 AD, he dispatched a monk named Augustine to bring the pagan Saxons into the Roman Christian fold.

Despite embracing the Christian missionary ethic, the Celtic Christians of southern Britain had made no attempt to convert the Saxons.[8] The gentler aspects of Christian doctrine failed to convince the Celts to love the enemies they hated so vehemently. They believed that the best revenge for Saxon brutality in this life was to let them burn in hell during the next life.[9] As a result, when Augustine landed in England, the Saxons were still almost entirely pagan.[10]

Augustine was apparently unaware that Celtic Christianity was flourishing in Ireland, Scotland, and isolated pockets of Britain.[11] But he did know of the fierce reputation of the Saxons. Prior to crossing the English Channel, he and his companions lost their courage and turned back, fearing a bloody reception in Kent. But he received direct orders to continue on his mission from Gregory I.[12]

Augustine was a Benedictine, a member of the monastic order founded by Benedict of Nursia. Established a half century before at Monte Cassino in Italy, the Benedictines did not embrace the harsh lifestyle of the ascetic monks in Egypt and Ireland. Instead they emphasized moderation in all things with an equal balance of work, prayer, and scholarship. They did not believe in the complete autonomy of their abbots. They submitted to an ecclesiastical chain of command linking them directly with the Bishop of Rome. Gregory I was himself a Benedictine and frequently employed his fellow monks for dangerous undertakings much as a king would dispatch a dedicated warrior sodality to challenge an enemy.[13] Despite Augustine's reluctance to set foot in Saxon lands, his pseudo-military monastic training eventually forced him to bow to the wishes of his superiors.

Gregory I had a special interest in Britain. He had been scheduled for a mission to the Saxons, but his election as Bishop of Rome interrupted his plans. Two years before Augustine's departure, he ordered the purchase of Saxon slave boys to act as interpreters for the Christians.[14] But Augustine left them behind, opting instead for Frankish priests who did not speak the Saxon tongue. Perhaps this was to please Bertha, the Frankish Christian princess who was married to Ethelbert, King of the Kentish Saxons.[15]

When Augustine arrived in Britain, he was welcomed by Queen Bertha and her personal chaplain, Bishop Luidhard, who had accompanied her to Kent. Presumably, Bertha and Luidhard worked in concert to make Ethelbert more receptive to the Roman Christian message. After some initial reluctance, the Saxon king accepted baptism from Augustine. Although the historian Bede later claimed that Ethelbert did not force his followers to become Christian, the example of a monarch had great influence on the behaviour of his subjects in a pyramidal social hierarchy. Large numbers of Kentish Saxons soon adopted Christianity.

Augustine did not immediately tamper with the traditional customs and practices of the Saxons. In a letter from Gregory I, he received instructions to retain any pagan belief or ritual which he deemed proper, incorporating them into the English Christian practices.[16] With this expedient policy, Gregory I protected Augustine's tenuous foothold in England by postponing the inevitable confrontation between the Saxon way of life and Roman Christian doctrine until Christianity was firmly entrenched in Saxon culture. From Gregory's perspective, it was a temporary compromise with evil designed to ultimately enhance the worldly power of good.

To reward Augustine's success, Gregory I named him the first Archbishop of Canterbury. In order to strengthen his central control over the Roman Christian sect, Gregory frequently attempted to frustrate the local election of bishops. Whenever possible, he tried to influence the balloting towards his own candidates. And in newly converted pagan lands with no established Christian community, he appointed bishops directly to prevent the development of an alternative method to select native religious leaders.[17]

While Augustine was consolidating his position among the Saxons, he discovered the existence of the Celtic Christians. With arrogance, he summoned the Celtic bishops of Britain and Ireland to appear before him, ignoring the fact that he resided among their enemies. When he met with the Celtic representatives, he demanded that they abandon any custom or practice deviating from the doctrines advocated by the Bishop of Rome.[18] He viewed the Celts as a rival Christian sect, as agents of evil. And since they posed no physical threat to Augustine, perhaps he felt that he could bully them into submission, ignoring Gregory's directive to temporarily endorse non-Roman rituals which were 'godly and righteous.'[19] When the Celtic bishops refused to acknowledge his authority, he prophesied military doom for the Celts, a fairly safe prediction considering how poorly the war with the Saxons was progressing.[20] In this confrontation, Augustine unsuccessfully attempted to wield both spiritual and temporal power to control an adversary.

Politically, Augustine was shrewd to alienate the Celtic Christians. The Saxons were an unpredictable warrior people and any hint of collusion with their enemies might earn him an unpleasant martyrdom. And since it was Gregory's official policy not to initially tamper with the practices and behaviours of the Saxons, a Celtic Christian purist might prematurely reveal the confrontational power paradigms of Christianity. The wrong words spoken to the wrong Saxon warlord might endanger the entire Roman Christian mission to England. In addition, Augustine probably believed that the Saxon success on the field of battle indicated that the destiny of Britain no longer lay among the Celts.

From the Celtic point of view, Augustine the Roman Christian bishop probably could not be distinguished from his Saxon associates. He had taken up residence in the heartland of the despised enemy, counselling their king and queen. He did not admonish the Saxons for their cruelty towards the Celts. Instead, he legitimatized their customs, incorporating them into Christian ritual. And he encouraged the Saxons to pursue the war against the Celts. Because of Augustine's behaviour, the Celts probably viewed submission to the Roman Christians as a prelude to Saxon political domination of all the Celtic lands.

In 604 AD, Augustine died and Laurentis was appointed the Archbishop of Canterbury. As time passed, the various Saxon kingdoms gradually adopted the Roman version of Christianity. The loose relationship between the Saxons and Roman Christianity continued to anger the Celts, adding to their unwillingness to compromise with the Bishop of Rome. Eventually, the two branches of Christianity clashed directly at the Synod of Whitby held in 664 AD.

In the early years of the seventh century AD, the military success of the Picts and the Dál Riatan Celts halted the northwards expansion of the Saxons. Because of their battlefield prowess, the Celts of northern Britain were less fearful of the foreign invaders than the southern clans.[21] The abbots of the monastery at Iona viewed their Saxon neighbours in the kingdom of Northumbria not as a threat, but as an opportunity to expand their power by converting them to the Christian religion. Dynastic quarrels among the Saxons provided the means for Celtic missionaries to infiltrate the royal court.

In 534 AD, a Saxon warlord named Oswald seized control of the Northumbrian throne. He had only a marginal claim to the crown. His father, Aethelfrith, had been king of Bernica. He had deposed Prince Edwin of Deira and created Northumbria by uniting the two realms under his rule. But after Aethelfrith died in battle, Edwin gained the crown of Northumbria and young Oswald was forced to flee to Celtic Dál Riata for safety. He probably studied at Iona, finding refuge among the island monks. Eventually, he became a Christian and returned to Northumbria to recapture the throne after Edwin was slain in battle.[22]

Once crowned as king, Oswald invited missionaries from Iona into his land to convert the people. Since the Celts did not speak the Saxon tongue, Oswald himself often acted as their interpreter, visibly demonstrating his royal approval of the religion.[23] The Celts convinced many Northumbrians to adopt their version of Christianity and built large monasteries at Whitby and Lindisfarne. When Oswald died in battle in 642 AD, his brother Oswiu succeeded him and continued the process of Christian conversion. But the success of Celtic Christianity in Northumbria was particularly galling to the Roman Christians. They had tried to penetrate Northumbria when

Edwin was king only to flee after Oswald captured the throne.[24] The expanding power of the Celts in the north was a potential threat to Roman Christian ecclesiastical domination of England. The Archbishop of Canterbury countered by sending his own priests to Northumbria. In the confrontational style of Christians, the two sects bickered and feuded, challenging each other on issues great and small. Eventually, Oswiu grew distressed by the public dissention among the Christians. He convened a synod at the monastery of Whitby to permanently resolve the dispute.

Oswiu's wife, Eanfled, followed the Roman Christian sect. She arranged for her son to be tutored by Wilfred, a Saxon priest who had been trained at the Celtic monastery of Lindisfarne but adopted the beliefs of the Roman Christians after a journey to Italy.[25] It was likely that Eanfled and Wilfred added to Oswiu's burdens by demanding that he acknowledge Roman Christianity as superior to the Celtic version.

At the synod, the defenders of the Celts were Coleman, the abbot of Lindisfarne, Hilda, the Abbess of Whitby, and Bishop Cedd who acted as interpreter. Wilfred and Agilbert of Wessex represented the Roman side. The main issues under discussion were the appropriate date of Easter and the shape of the Celtic tonsure. But these minor matters served to mask the true agenda of the synod which focused on the absolute authority of the Bishop of Rome to wield power over all Christians. During the debate, Coleman cited the authority of Columcille and the practices of St. John as the basis for Celtic customs. But Wilfred refuted his argument with the gospel passage 'Thou art Peter and upon this rock, I will build my Church,' which he claimed gave the Bishop of Rome unlimited power over all Christians.[26] Unfortunately for the Celts, Coleman did not challenge the validity of the passage or the self-serving interpretation adopted by the Bishop of Rome. He merely agreed that these words were indeed found in scripture. Oswiu immediately ruled in favour of the Roman Christian position, requiring the Celts in his kingdom to follow all rules of ritual and doctrine required by the Bishop of Rome.[27]

The record of the judgement at Whitby was written many

years later by the Venerable Bede, a Roman Christian monk who viewed the confrontation as a triumph of the righteous power of the Bishop of Rome. But the Celts felt otherwise. Unable to submit to foreign ecclesiastical domination, Coleman resigned as the Abbot of Lindisfarne and returned to Iona along with his Celtic monks. Some years later, he emigrated to western Ireland where he founded a monastery far from the Roman Christian sphere of interest. Hilda remained as Abbess of Whitby until her death in 680 AD and continued to support the Celtic version of Christianity despite Oswiu's decree.[28] Over the next several centuries, the influence of the Celts over Saxon Christians gradually diminished.

The Synod of Whitby did not mark the end of the Celtic Christian Church. But it did signal the beginning of the end. In a direct confrontation with a rival Christian sect, the Celts were unable to effectively wield political power to achieve a result favourable to their cause. This reinforced Roman Christian claims that the Celts were deviant, heretical, and inspired by the devil. It also gave religious sanction for the Saxons to continue warring against the Celts during the centuries to come.

*

In a letter to the Thessalonians, Paul said, 'This is the will of God ... that you should abstain from fornication'.[29] Together with the writings of later Christian philosophers, this statement helped to place sexuality in the realm of evil and abstinence in the realm of good. In theory, ardent Christians rarely compromised with the evil of sexuality. Physical intimacy was permissible only for the purposes of procreation and celibacy was a more desirable condition than marriage. But in practice, the more pragmatic Christian sects appeared to recognize an additional permissible use of sexuality to establish and maintain temporal power.

The Roman Christians were particularly proficient at placing desirable women in royal household. One of the principal objectives of these wives and concubines appeared to be the conversion of kings to the Roman version of the Christian faith. The beautiful Clotilda convinced the Frankish king Clovis to abandon his pagan beliefs and acknowledge the Christian doctrines of the Bishop of Rome. After her death, the Roman Christians honoured her persuasive ability by making her a saint.[30] Theodolinda was married to two successive Lombard kings, Autharis and Agilulf. She influenced both to reject Arian Christianity in favour of the Roman version.[31] In Kent, Bertha prompted her royal husband Ethelbert to heed the words of the Roman Christian missionary, Augustine. And in Northumbria, Ethelburga brought to her marriage with Edwin the Roman priest Paulinus 'as if he had been the companion of their carnal union.'[32]

If the relationships between these husbands and wives were purely contractual and motivated by dynastic gain alone, the men would not have been so willing to adopt the Roman Christian beliefs of their marriage partners. The women probably bartered their sexual charms to sway the convictions of their husbands. Such bedroom pleasures would have been a pleasant bonus to any wealth or alliances offered by the Bishop of Rome. The surviving records of the time did not clearly indicate whether the placement of women in royal bedchambers was a far reaching conspiracy or merely random good fortune. But when Boniface V was the Bishop of Rome, he sent Ethelburga a letter encouraging her to use whatever means necessary to convert her husband, Edwin. Along with his directive, he presented her with a silver mirror and an ivory comb.[33] The gifts were designed to enhance her sexual desirability and seemed to suggest the tactics Ethelburga should pursue in her efforts to convert Edwin. The Bishop of Rome was the beneficiary of the bedroom abilities of women like Ethelburga, transforming their sexual power over their partners into political power for himself.

In comparison with the Roman Christians, the Celts were politically naive with little appreciation for the intrigue necessary to make bloodless conquests over pagans and other Christian sects. The decentralized administrative paradigms of the Celtic Christians were not well suited for empire building. And they did not seem to grasp the potential for political power latent in sexuality. They offered pagans and their Roman rivals no Christian version of Queen Maev who artfully employed her body to entice allies and influence the outcome of battles.

The Christian Celts clung to an exclusively confrontational approach to the interrelationship between power and sexuality. Ascetic monks who struggled to maintain their celibacy feuded with political figures who indulged their sexual appetites. The monks assumed that the authority of their religious beliefs would be sufficient to overcome the temporal power of kings and queens. They were usually wrong.

Crime and Sexuality

In pre-Christian Celtic society, law reflected actual human behaviour, embodying the customs and practices of the local community. In sexual matters, the law recognized the legitimacy of a wide range of possible relationships and activities. Beyond prohibiting violence and fraud, Celtic law givers seemed to appreciate their own inability to dictate the limits of acceptable sexual behaviour.

In Ireland, the traditional legal system was called Brehon, an English corruption of the Irish word for judge, *breitheamh.* The Irish system survived until the English gained complete political control of the island in the seventeenth century AD. In Britain, the Celts developed an analogous system called the Molmutine Laws named after a legendary Prince of Cornwall, Dunwallo Molmutius.[1] But the Celtic law in Britain died out shortly after the Saxon invasions. The Welsh created the Laws of Hywel Dda which functioned until the fourteenth century.

The Celtic judicial codes were based on the traditions of the extended family clan known as the *tuath* and were virtually unchangeable. A judge was allowed only to comment on the law, applying it to the circumstances of a particular case. Once a decision was rendered, compliance was usually voluntary. If enforcement was necessary, the duty fell to the kin of the aggrieved party.

In attempts to achieve a measure of legal uniformity, some of the High Kings of Ireland believed there should also be national laws. Through a process of consensus with the leaders of the Irish clans, they devised the *Cáin,* or the law of all the land. But in cases where the *Cáin* conflicted with the customs of the community, the local law superseded the national law.[2]

Originally, the laws of the Celts were transmitted orally and required verbatim memorization by the brehon judges. After the development of writing, scribes recorded the laws in tracts which varied according to the local community which the law served. In the timeless tradition of lawyers, the scribes preserved the ancient Irish language employed by the brehons, an outmoded form of speech understood poorly in the eighth and ninth centuries AD. They provided glosses to help with interpretation, but even the notes were often inaccurate.[3] The result was confusion which weakened the ability of the Brehon Law to function effectively.

In Celtic society, each person belonged to a class. In the highest position were the nobles, people of great value to the community. In the lowest position were the bondservants, people who contributed little to the community. If a person committed a crime against another, the status of the aggrieved party dictated the degree of penalty. But the Brehon Law was impartial, judging the misdeeds of kings and beggars with the same measure of severity. To restore damaged honour, the criminal paid the honour-price. This was a quantity of goods fixed in accordance with the victim's rank in society. If the crime was particularly outrageous, the judge added a punitive fine called a *dire*. The Celts placed murder in a separate category with a very large monetary penalty termed the *eric*. The kin of the wrongdoer were collectively responsible for the payment of any judgement.[4] If the criminal's family refused to pay the fine, the aggrieved party often fasted in front of the offender's house. This was a tactic designed to bring shame upon the lawbreaker and force payment of the damages.[5] If the criminal still refused to pay, the kin of the victim could seize goods equal to the fine, a gambit which frequently led to blood feuds between clans.

Sexual crimes against the individual occupied a broad area of Celtic law. The brehons considered the mutilation of a man by the amputation of his penis outrageous and demanded the full honour-price and a punitive *dire*. Castration alone required only the *dire*, somehow not affecting a man's honour as much as the loss of his penis. Despite the relatively high status accorded to women in Celtic society, the Brehon Law did not address the mutilation of female genitalia or breasts.[6] But strangely enough, if a man forcibly shaved the pubic hair of an unwilling woman, he was liable for her full honour-price and *dire*.

The Brehon Law distinguished heterosexual rape by violence from rape by deceit. In violent rape, the woman was due an honour-price and *dire*. Rape by deceit occurred if the victim was asleep or drunk and unable to give her consent. The law treated it less seriously than violent rape, requiring only the payment of the honour-price as restitution. In the Celtic matrilinear society, children belonged to the clan of the mother. But this did not relieve the rapist from the burden of support for any child born from his crime.

The Brehon Law did not address prostitution in the modern sense of bartering sexual favours for gold. But it did view harshly a woman who allowed all and sundry to sleep with her. The law defined her as a 'bush-harlot', as a woman who made love with three or four men in the course of one night in a secluded spot. There was no penalty given for this behaviour, but if the 'bush-harlot' sought legal redress for a wrong, she had no honour-price regardless of her status in society.[7] This allowed men to challenge a female accuser on the basis of her previous sexual conduct.

The Brehon Law did not attempt to dictate who could form sexual relationships. Incest was not addressed. Since many mythic figures and Christian saints were born from sexual liaisons between close relatives, the early Celts probably did not consider incest to be criminal behaviour if both parties were willing. The Brehon Law also made no mention of an age of sexual consent and presumably adults were legally free to sleep with children.

The Celts viewed marriage as a social contract for the purposes of creating children. The Brehon Law recognized ten separate categories of the marital relationship. A man might have one wife or several. The first wife had higher status than the second who was termed the *ben-charrthach,* the loved woman. A man was also permitted to maintain a sexual relationship with a woman whom he did not permanently live with.[8]

Such complex romantic liaisons were probably available only to those men able to brave the domestic disputes which they would inevitably trigger. But the object of the Brehon Law was to recognize the variations of human behaviour without condemnation. So the law gave a three day grace period to a wife after she discovered her husband's interest in another woman. She could indulge her jealousy in any manner she chose, assaulting her husband or his new lover without legal penalty.[9]

The Brehon Law was first recorded in the eighth and ninth centuries AD and did not mention the possibility of multiple marriage partners for women. Yet Roman and Greek observers claimed they encountered polyandrous relationships among the Celts. And Irish mythic figures such as Maev and Cessair were women who appeared to enjoy intimacy with many men. It was possible that the early Celtic custom of polyandry had withered by the time Christian scribes recorded the laws and they omitted any reference to women with several husbands as irrelevant.

Divorce was permitted for both parties in a marriage based on a variety of circumstances generally focused on fertility. A woman could divorce her husband if he were clearly barren, impotent, or very fat. The Celts believed that extreme male obesity was a barrier to efficient lovemaking and placed an intolerable burden on the female partner. If a husband revealed his wife's intimate secrets to another, or displayed such sexual desire for other men or boys that his wife was deprived of his conjugal services, she could divorce him.[10] Abandonment by her husband was additional grounds enabling a woman to obtain a divorce. But if a wife abandoned her husband, she was considered outlaw, a person without kin and not entitled to the protection of the law. A man could divorce a woman if she refused sexual relations with him or indulged indiscreetly in sexual relations with others. Both husband and wife could find no fault grounds for divorce in debilitating illness, serious injury which made sex impossible, insanity, or a journey which would take one partner away for an extended period.

Since the Celts regarded marriage as a contract for a specific purpose, it did not affect the rights of women in any way. They could own property, engage in a profession, and freely make financial agreements separate from their husbands. As long as she continued to provide sexual services to her spouse, a woman could swear an oath against him and make alliances with his enemies.

Husbands considered flagrant adultery by their wives as a shaming commentary on their sexual abilities. Men believed that if they were sufficiently skilful in satisfying the sexual needs of their wives, women would have no cause to look elsewhere. The wife's lover could add to the husband's shame by offering to buy any offspring produced in the adulterous relationship by paying an honour-price to the husband in accordance with the status of the child.

Despite the trend of the Brehon Law to sanction a wide array of actual human sexual behaviour, it also served to shape the values of the community. By authorizing certain behaviour, the law tended to encourage it. By prohibiting other behaviour, the law tended to discourage it. The result was a subtle interchange of values as the Brehon Law both reflected and created the sexual ethics of the Celts.

*

Christian legal philosophy diverged sharply from the Brehon system. Instead of responding to human behaviour, the Christians appeared to view law as a means to channel conduct into the ideal patterns demanded by dogma. The head of the religious community was the law giver, judge, and enforcer with authority springing from divine right. Although converts gave their implied consent to the Christian system by accepting baptism, consensus among the governed was not considered a legitimate basis of legal power.

Despite Christ's rejection of the legalism represented by the

Pharisees in his own society, the ecclesiastical institutions created by the early Christians had to establish internal rules of management for their followers.[11] As these institutions grew more complex and interfaced with the pagan world, the Christians developed their own vision of law and government. Borrowing heavily from Roman and Eastern Mediterranean paradigms, they gradually embraced an authoritarian legal system which validated the right of a central authority to make and enforce law. Legal power was created at the top of a political hierarchy and flowed downward to the people.

Initially, Christian legal philosophy did not have a great impact on the Brehon system. The new perception of law was confined to monasteries where the abbot or abbess made rules called penitentials to govern their cloistered followers. Because the early Celtic Christians mimicked the decentralized structure of their society, the penitentials were not uniform. Their content depended on the doctrinal interpretations of individual religious leaders. But as the new faith became more established, the penitentials began to apply to lay Christians who lived outside the monastery. By the eighth century AD, the Celtic people found themselves in a society with parallel legal systems. Both the Brehon Laws and the Christian penitentials demanded loyalty, yet each set of laws offered an opposing view of the nature of criminal behaviour.

In sexual matters, the penitentials diverged sharply from the traditional Celtic philosophy of law. The Christian code was based on a norm for sexual behaviour which evolved outside of the Celtic community.[12] In addition to penalizing acts of sexual violence, it criminalized solitary and consensual activity such as masturbation, fellatio, and cunnilingus which caused no objective harm to an individual or community. A private agreement to modify the marriage contract to exclude fertility while retaining sex was not possible under the Christian system. The penitentials also emphasized physical chastisement for violations, a concept alien to the Brehon Law which stressed reparations to the injured. Since many Christian crimes had no victim, the degree of penance depended on the social status of the wrongdoer. An abbot who made love with a married woman received a far more severe penalty than a cowherd who engaged in the same behaviour.

The Synod of Patrick was one of the earliest penitentials and was composed long after the saint's death. It created categories of sexual crime based on relationship, forbidding divorce and casual lovers to married men and women. It also prohibited vowed male and female celibates from acting in any manner that might lead to suspicions of sexual impropriety. The primary penalty was excommunication from the Christian community.[13]

By the end of the sixth century AD, Finnian's Penitential gained widespread acceptance in monasteries.[14] Perhaps finding that the Synod of Patrick had cast too many Christians out of the community because of their sexual inclinations, Finnian's rule stressed physical punishment. The penance usually involved flogging followed by many years of semi-starvation. It included a comprehensive list of forbidden sexual relationships and detailed specific activities prohibited even if the relationship was proper.

Cummean's Penitential was composed in the seventh century AD and devoted particular attention to homosexual activity between men. Cataloguing virtually every potential sexual variation, it levied a degree of penalty depending on the extent of homosexual contact. Passionate kissing earned eight fasts, but a simple kiss only six. Mutual masturbation and interfemoral stimulation received several years of reduced rations. Cummean reserved the most severe punishment of seven years atonement for anal intercourse.[15]

The harshness of the penitentials for sexual transgressions demonstrated the personal conflict facing Christian Celts who lived in a land with two incongruous legal systems. If one spouse chose divorce under the Brehon Law, the penitentials forbade either spouse from forming another sexual relationship. In cases of rape, the Brehon Law granted the victim financial restitution. Under the penitentials, the victim had to be content with the infliction of corporal punishment on the rapist. No mechanism existed in Celtic society for the resolution of conflicts between the two legal systems.

*

Because the Christians believed that their viewpoint was the only correct one, they gradually sought to replace the Brehon system with their own. But as long as the Christians remained a minority sect among the Celts, they did not have sufficient power to openly challenge the Brehon Law. The first serious attempt to graft Christian values onto the Brehon system came in 697 AD with the adoption of a *Cáin* sponsored by Adomnán, an Abbot of Iona.

Adomnán was a prominent scholar of his time who compiled a biography of Columcille and wrote a travelogue of the Holy Land. He was the first Abbot of Iona to abandon the Celtic version of Christianity and submit to the authority and doctrines of the Bishop of Rome.[16] The national law he advocated put women, children, and clergy under religious protection in time of war. It was roughly modelled on a Roman Christian edict gaining popularity in Europe known as the *lex innocentium,* the law of the innocent. In accordance with Celtic custom, the *Cáin Adomnán* was adopted by a consensus of clan chiefs and became the law of all the land after ratification by the High King.

As justification for the fundamental changes in custom required by the *Cáin Adomnán*, its preamble suggested that women in Celtic society lived in wretched conditions. According to Adomnán, unwilling naked women were commonly forced to provide domestic and sexual service to coarse male warriors in banquet halls. Brutal husbands frequently flogged their reluctant wives to drive them into the forefront of battle lines, indifferent to wounds or suffering.

The practices Adomnán sought to alter probably took place regularly in Celtic society, but their need for remedy depended on point of view. Women did indeed fight alongside men in battle, and it would not have been unusual for warriors of both genders to engage in sexual relations before and after combat. But literature and historical chronicles provided little evidence that women were forced into battle or sexual encounters.

In traditional Celtic society, women enjoyed a relatively high status. Their right to bear arms was a duty and a source of pride, despite the physical risks of combat. And any man who sexually assaulted a woman warrior would have to contend with her sword as well as the Brehon Law prohibiting rape.[17]

Adomnán's Roman Christian sensitivities were apparently outraged by the customs of his people sanctioning rampant sexuality in military camps and the equality of gender inherent in the concept of women warriors. No Christian woman who modelled her life after Mary or Brigid could properly engage in such activities. Yet the society expected this behaviour from her. To align Celtic custom with Christian values, Adomnán attempted to modify the expectations of the society from the top down, using the *Cáin* as the vehicle for change.

By granting women a religious immunity from military service, the new law served to reduce some of the personal conflict felt by Christian women living in a society still largely governed by druid customs. No longer would they have to risk death in battle or sexual adventure in army camps. But women had to pay a price for their new status as members of a victim class protected by law. The *Cáin* assessed a quarterly tax on women according to their means, payable to the monks of Iona.[18] If Christian women failed in their duty of support, Adomnán prophesied that their children would decay. This final part of the *Cáin Adomnán* which depended on the ability of women to allocate wealth seemed to refute the earlier passage depicting conditions similar to slavery.

Adomnán's law assumed that women were incapable of determining their own destiny and therefore needed the protection of a societal institution. It sought to prohibit women from engaging in the profession of warrior, a time-honoured role for Celtic females. It was the beginning of Christian-inspired restrictions for Celtic women which would ultimately ban them from the traditional occupations of healer, scholar, and judge.

But a substantial number of Celts ignored the new statute. It had to be reenacted many times, indicating that the law was not widely observed.[19] Yet as centuries elapsed, the ability of the Christians to influence civil law grew. Although they continuously maintained an ecclesiastical legal system to discipline Christians for religious infractions, they managed to secure an increasing amount of civil legislation reflecting their values. In the late eleventh century AD, the King of Munster, Tairrdelbach ó Bríen, changed the Brehon marriage laws to conform with Roman Christian doctrine after urging by Pope Gregory VII and the Archbishop of Canterbury.[20]

After the Anglo-Norman invasions introduced English Common Law to Ireland, the Brehon Laws slowly fell into disuse in the territory administered by the conquerors.

The transition towards the Christian philosophy of law in Celtic lands seemed to coincide with the development of urban centres. The Brehon Law with its emphasis on community was suited for an agricultural society. But the ties with ancient tradition gradually eroded in Dublin, Limerick, Galway, and Cork when large numbers of people were attracted to city life. The new urban environments were a polyglot mixture of Celts, Norse settlers, and traders from all parts of Europe. To effectively govern the behaviour of people who were not united by a common heritage, the cities needed a new legal outlook stressing central authority and swift enforcement. And the Christians provided a ready made legal system tailored to urban needs.

The spread of literacy also aided Christian law in its competition with the Brehon system. The native laws were oral, given weight by Celtic society's esteem for the oral tradition. But as literacy spread, reverence for the written word slowly eclipsed respect for the spoken word. The earliest surviving Celtic legal text is the *Collectio Canonum Hiberensis* compiled in the early eighth century AD. It not only sets down Christian rules but details their application to Celtic society.[21] As the number of written laws grew, they were widely distributed providing Christians with an authoritative basis for disputing the validity of the Brehon system.

As the prominence of the Brehon Laws gradually eroded, the Christian code found itself unable to fully govern sexuality. The activities of lovers in the privacy of the bed chamber remained beyond the control of civil or ecclesiastical officials. Transgressions would come to light only if a party complained. By forbidding certain relationships and behaviours, the Christian rules seemed to make sexual adventure all the more attractive.

Invasions, Brothels and Witches

In 1152 AD, an Irish sexual relationship helped to set in motion a chain of events which would forever alter Celtic society. A forty year old woman named Devorgilla tired of her elderly husband, Tiernán ó Rourke, King of Bréifne. She abandoned him to live with Dermot mac Murrough, a man closer to her own age who may have had a sexual relationship with her before her marriage to Tiernán.[1] If the ancient customs had still been in force, Devorgilla could have merely sued for divorce and married her new lover, avoiding the social stigma of abandonment. If she did not want to take such a permanent step, she could have had an adulterous affair with Dermot which her husband would probably ignore rather than face public shame for his inability to meet his wife's needs. But in the centuries after Adomnán sponsored his *Cáin*, Celtic sexual practices had gradually changed, conforming more closely to Christian standards. Reform of the Celtic marriage laws made divorce difficult to obtain and adultery illegal. Abandonment was the only option available to Devorgilla to indulge her passions and remedy marital unhappiness.

Dermot was the King of Leinster, a man with enough power to bend the law. And to protect Devorgilla's honour and her legal status, he created a fiction that he kidnapped her, taking her to his bed against her will. But all accounts agree that she was an eager accomplice to her staged abduction. For a year, the two lovers enjoyed each other's company. But unfortunately for Dermot, Devorgilla eventually wearied of his tyrannical and jealous nature and returned to her husband.[2] Tiernán ó Rourke believed his wife's tale of imprisonment and rape. He swore a blood oath against Dermot, vowing an eternal feud with the man who had stolen Devorgilla's sexual honour.

The attitudes of Devorgilla's two lovers implied a dramatic shift in the status of Celtic women. Although Devorgilla appeared to exercise some degree of control over her own sexuality, Tiernán and Dermot fought over her as if her wishes and desires were immaterial. Each man blamed the other for Devorgilla's choices, believing that her sexuality was theirs to control.

Tiernán's hatred for Dermot smouldered until 1166 AD when he backed Rory ó Connor's successful bid for the High Kingship of Ireland. To repay his loyal supporter, the new High King formed a coalition to wage war on Dermot mac Murrough, defeating him in battle and driving him from Ireland. Dermot fled to England, to the court of Henry II.[3]

Henry must have wondered what to make of the deposed Irish king and the ragtag retinue accompanying him into exile. Among the elegant Norman nobles, the rustic sheepskin clothes and drooping moustaches of the Celts probably seemed quite odd. But Henry was an astute politician who recognized opportunity. In the Bull *Laudibiliter*, he already had papal approval to unleash his knights on Ireland. And the arrival of Dermot requesting aid to regain a lost throne provided the political excuse to acquire new territory while solving the nagging problem of land ownership among the Anglo-Norman nobility.

In England, Henry was gradually eliminating the practice of subinfeudiation which divided a lord's holdings among all his male heirs. The plots of land were becoming too small to generate enough wealth for the lords to meet their feudal obligations to the king. So Henry began to introduce primogeniture, making the eldest son the sole heir to his father's estates.[4] The disinherited younger sons had scant prospects of leading a life of comfort and prosperity in their homeland. So Henry gave Dermot permission to recruit an army of Anglo-Norman knights from the sons of the noble families who had ambitions to own Irish estates.

Dermot found allies among the lords of southern Wales, engaging the interest of the FitzGeralds, FitzHenries and the Carews. To gain the support of Richard FitzGilbert de Clare, called Strongbow, Dermot promised him the hand of his beautiful daughter, Aife. In May of 1169, the Anglo-Normans landed a force of thirty knights at Bannow in Wexford. They were supported by over three hundred horsemen and archers, mostly of Flemish origin. Dermot soon joined them with five hundred of his loyal Leinstermen.

Initially, the Irish High King ignored the intruders. Many different races had come to Ireland in the past without creating a major threat to the Celtic way of life. But as the Anglo-Norman holdings spread northward and westward, the High King gathered an army to repel the invaders. But instead of war, Strongbow offered compromise. He promised that the Anglo-Normans would return to their homeland if Dermot's title was restored. Eager to avoid a pitched battle with the heavily armoured knights, the High King quickly agreed.

But Strongbow was merely negotiating for time. He was soon reinforced by another two hundred knights and a thousand men at arms. He marched on Dublin and then on Ossory, gaining control of a substantial portion of southern Ireland. And the High King was unable to muster a force strong enough to repel the invaders.

When King Henry himself arrived in 1171 with an army of four thousand, he was welcomed by a substantial body of Celtic Roman Christians who believed the English would correct any doctrines or practices deviating from Roman dogma. In the century preceding the invasion, the number of Celtic Christians who leaned towards rule by Rome had increased until they were a powerful force in Ireland. In the southern part of the island, many Christians acknowledged the Archbishop of Canterbury as their ecclesiastical superior and instituted a series of religious reforms that brought them into closer alignment with Roman doctrine.

In military terms, the Anglo-Norman invasion was only a moderate success. Henry accepted the feudal submission of many Irish kings, giving him theoretical control of most of the

island. But the Irish Celts did not fully understand the implications of the ritual, viewing it as a formality to secure an
alliance with a powerful neighbour. The Celts living beyond
the territory directly controlled by the Anglo-Normans did not
perceive Henry as their rightful overlord. But the newcomers
did not immediately press their claims of sovereignty. They
abandoned warfare, established a manorial system to farm the
land and imported workers from Wales. The nobles built castles and created a hierarchy of fiefdoms owing allegiance to the
English throne. The Anglo-Norman territory became known as
the Pale, an area where English law and custom conflicted
directly with the traditional Celtic way of life.

Unlike the Saxon invasion of Britain almost eight hundred
years before, the Anglo-Norman presence in Ireland did not
immediately hurl Celtic society into turmoil and crises. The
invaders appeared to have limited objectives, focusing on creating an English feudal system in the territory they controlled.
And to exert political influence over the Celtic region beyond
the Pale, they offered noble titles and stipends to the Irish clan
chiefs in return for nominal fealty to the English crown. But
the Celtic way of life had an unexpected effect on the invaders.
After a century, many of the Anglo-Normans adopted native
customs, riding horses bareback, wearing Irish fashions and
speaking the Celtic tongue. Intermarriages were common and
after several generations many inhabitants of the Pale boasted
of mixed blood. By the beginning of the fourteenth century AD,
the Anglo-Normans had lost so much of their original charac-
ter they became known as the Anglo-Irish.[5]

Despite the common influence of Christianity, the sexual
viewpoints of the Anglo-Normans differed from the Celts. The
society of England reflected the recent fusion of Saxon and
French values, developing institutions and attitudes closely
modelled on the ideas permeating continental Europe. Love
was divorced from sexuality, existing in a spiritual sphere
distant from the sordid details of sex. A great gulf of communication opened between the genders as men overlaid a courtly
ideal of nonsexual love on noblewomen while reserving their
sexual expressions for women they regarded as base born. But

in all strata of society, illicit sexual relationships were rampant as men and women discreetly ignored the standards of Christian sexual behaviour. In the Pale, the Anglo-Normans continued the sexual practices of their homeland which made them privately promiscuous and publicly chaste.

*

By the late Medieval period, organized prostitution flourished in most parts of England. It provided a necessary outlet for suppressed sexuality in a society outwardly aspiring to the difficult ideals of virginity and chastity. Virtually every town boasted of a bawdy house enjoying the protection of the local noble, bishop or abbot. By charging the prostitutes a percentage of their fees, the civil and ecclesiastical authorities received a sizeable annual revenue. In return, they insured that any laws barring prostitution were enforced only against those women who plied their trade in the streets, reducing competition for the quasi-official brothels.[6] To avoid scandalous charges brought by political enemies, the nobles and clergymen who controlled the houses of prostitution often leased them to men of lesser distinction to oversee the management.[7]

During the reign of Henry II, brothels had become so widespread that the crown issued an ordinance regulating the activities of prostitutes and their relationship with the owners of the brothels. The law prohibited the employment of nuns and women who were married or visibly pregnant. The prostitutes could not go into the streets to solicit, but could tempt passers-by from doorways and windows. The county bailiff was ordered to make regular inspections to insure that any forbidden practices were curbed.[8]

Organized prostitution had languished after the fall of Rome. But about the time of Charlemagne, it enjoyed a revival on the feudal estates of France and Germany. Unmarried women of the serf class were quartered separately on the estate, a constant source of temptation for the lord and his guests. Some women were willing to barter their sexual favours in return for a privileged position. And those who were unwilling had little choice but to succumb to the advances of a powerful noble.[9] As towns developed in the later Middle Ages, the concept of a ready and waiting pool of women available for sexual pleasure was transferred to the brothel. The term itself comes from the Old English word for wretch, perhaps referring to the living conditions of the women who worked in the houses of prostitution.[10] Because the towns had a more commercial orientation than the manor and were not usually under the control of a single noble, money was exchanged for a sexual encounter with women employed by the brothel.

The basis of prostitution during the later Medieval period was deeply rooted in the feudal system. Women of the lower class could avoid a life of toil and drudgery by bartering their sexuality, despite the risk of disease. Nuns and married women of the upper classes could escape the confines of their life by secretly entering a brothel, as testified to by the laws prohibiting their employment as prostitutes. As long as they profited from the brothels, the nobles and clergy turned a blind eye to the houses devoted to sexual adventure and were often found among the clientele.

The custom of the bawdy house was probably imported to Dublin, Wexford and the other Irish urban centres controlled by the English. The Anglo-Norman lords and Welsh immigrants who worked the farms in the Pale would have been fully acquainted with the concept of prostitution and brothels in their homeland. The laws of Henry II and subsequent rules regulating prostitution did have full effect in the Pale. And a few centuries after the Anglo-Norman invasions, the female operated 'ale-house' was a common feature in the Irish landscape, offering clients food, drink and a sexual romp with a woman.[11]

The existence of formal prostitution reflected the diminished status of women in feudal society. Few avenues for financial gain were open to women born without wealth or position. Men regarded women of the lower classes as drudges, camp followers and whores, as lesser beings whose sole purpose for existence was to serve. Prostitution became one of the only viable means for women to earn a living without backbreaking labour. But the prospects for independence among noble born women were equally as bleak. Because descent and inheritance among the Anglo-Normans were traced from the male ancestors, a noblewoman was often little more than an incubator for her husband's seed. Her sexuality had to be closely guarded to insure that her offspring indeed belonged to the husband. Neither group of women could fully control their own sexual destiny. The diminished position of women in feudal society was given religious approval by Christian scholars such as Albert the Great and Thomas Aquinas who claimed that women were constitutionally less qualified than men for moral behaviour.[12] Despite the political leadership offered by capable females like Eleanor of Aquitaine and Blanche of Castile, the thirteenth century saw the gradual erosion of the status of women across Europe.[13]

The feudal view of female sexuality was creeping into Celtic society despite their tradition of equality among the genders. The permanent presence of the Anglo-Irish and the frequency of intermarriage between the two peoples hastened the injection of the new sexual paradigms into Celtic society. For more than a century after Strongbow's invasion, a state of flux existed among the Celts and the Anglo-Irish as each society attempted to accommodate the viewpoints of the other.

*

By the early fourteenth century AD, two sets of sexual paradigms co-existed in Ireland. The Anglo-Irish attempted to follow the rules of sexual conduct imported from their homeland while the Celts clung to the practices inherited from their ancestors and modified by the Christians. Yet for the Anglo-Irish, the less restrictive Celtic way of life held an almost irresistible allure. Maidens mimicked their Celtic cousins by sitting astride their horses bareback and prematurely rupturing their hymens, the evidence of their virginity. Married women secretly passed the night in the arms of their paramours, ignoring the platonic ideals of courtly love which emphasized physical fidelity to their husbands. And in many

Anglo-Irish households, women behaved with a fierce independence regarded as scandalous by visitors from England.

The English clergy were the first to react to Anglo-Irish conduct in the Pale that they viewed as deviant. In 1317 AD, the Bishop of Ossory was a Franciscan friar named Richard de Ledrede. He convened a synod which purported to discover the existence of witchcraft in Ireland.[14] Since Christian mythology suggested that female witches far outnumbered male warlocks, the persecution of witches was a direct attempt to curb the behaviour of women whose attitudes and practices were an affront to Roman Christian sexual doctrine. After the accession of John XXII in 1316 AD to the papal throne then located in Avignon, de Ledrede had received directives indicating that witchcraft should be equated with heresy. At his synod, he initiated a feverous hunt for Irish witches in accordance with the Pope's instructions.[15]

The Roman Christians treated heresy far more severely in the fourteenth century AD than in the sixth century AD. By de Ledrede's time, their doctrine had gained such widespread acceptance that the Pope could authorize the use of unlimited force against any group or individual with different beliefs. By equating witchcraft with heresy, male religious authorities could legally employ whatever violence they deemed necessary against women whose conduct deviated from the Christian norm. And since witchcraft was a religious matter, de Ledrede believed himself above the English civil laws designed to prevent unjust prosecution and punishment.

De Ledrede's sudden discovery of witchcraft in the Pale advanced several objectives of the clergy. In the ongoing rivalry between church and state for legal supremacy, de Ledrede believed he was demonstrating that there was an evil in the world beyond the power of civil government to remedy. In addition, he could brand any people who clung to the ancient druid beliefs as witches, eliminating the last vestiges of the old religion in Ireland. And since witchcraft as defined by the Roman Christians usually had a sexual component, he could intimidate any woman who flaunted the behavioural rules of feudal society with uninhibited sexual expression.

De Ledrede's purpose and methods were alien to the democratic traditions of both the Celts and the Anglo-Irish. But de Ledrede was not concerned with opposition from clan chiefs and nobles. He dispatched a large number of Franciscan friars on a quest to ferret out the witches he was certain were hiding in his diocese. In 1324, the attention of the brown robed friars eventually focused on an Anglo-Irish woman of noble birth, Alice Kyteller.

Three of Alice's husbands had died of natural causes. Her fourth husband appeared quite mad and vocally blamed his mental instability on a magical potion administered by Alice. Possibly because of these accusations, de Ledrede's friars took many of Alice's friends into custody for questioning. As might be expected when faced with intimidation by the unlimited power of the Holy Inquisition, they made fantastic allegations against Alice to secure their own immunity. They claimed she poisoned her previous husbands, conjured spirits with animal entrails and had a demon lover named Robin mac Art.[16] It was possible that Alice knew and practised the traditional herbal medicine of the Celts which the friars would regard as sorcery. And if Robin mac Art was her Celtic paramour who came to her bed chamber at dusk and left at dawn, the friars might perceive him as the demon incubus of Christian mythology.

But when de Ledrede attempted to arrest Alice, he met with unexpected opposition from the Chancellor of Ireland who believed the accusations groundless. When de Ledrede persisted in his efforts to capture Alice, he was himself arrested. By using the power of interdict, by halting all religious services in his diocese, he secured his release. But Alice Kyteller quickly fled Ireland. And de Ledrede had to settle for the capture of Petronilla of Meath, her Celtic maid. After administering torture, he burned the unfortunate woman at the stake, the only ritual immolation of a witch ever to occur in Ireland.

In continental Europe during the fourteenth century AD, witch hysteria was one of the methods used by religious authorities to insure conformity. But the persecution of men and women without due legal process by the Church was repugnant to the democratic traditions embedded in both the

Celtic Brehon Law and the English Common Law. Fortunately, de Ledrede's successors abandoned their confrontation with the civil authorities over the matter of witchcraft in Ireland. Yet the potential threat created by the persecution of Alice Kyteller and the execution of Petronilla of Meath was likely to have had a chilling effect on the activities of women who wondered if they would be the next example made by the clergy.

In 1366 AD, King Edward III of England acted to curb the drift of Anglo-Irish behaviour towards the Celtic way of life. With his sponsorship, the London Parliament passed the Statutes of Kilkenny, making it a crime for the Anglo-Irish to adopt Celtic behaviours. They were forbidden to speak the Celtic tongue, to dress in native fashions, and even to ride a horse without a saddle. The laws also prohibited inter-marriage and casual sexual relationships between the Anglo-Irish and the Celts.[17]

The Statutes of Kilkenny attempted to assure the dominance of the Anglo-Norman way of life in Ireland. They were largely successful since no true merger of paradigms occurred between the two societies. During the next three hundred years, the English distanced themselves from the native culture of Ireland. They lived in their cities and castles leaving the countryside to the Celts who they increasingly perceived as rustic and uncouth. By war and intrigue, the English eventually extended their influence until the entire island was under their rule.

As the political independence of the Irish Celts eroded, so did their way of life. New ideas flooded their land, supported by English swords and English laws. Celtic sexual attitudes underwent their final transformation, aligning themselves more closely with the practices and beliefs common to Western Europe.

15

Final Fusion

During the centuries after the English invasion of Ireland, the distinct institutions and paradigms defining Celtic society gradually disappeared. Despite measures like the Statutes of Kilkenny, the Anglo-Irish and the Celts continued the process of cultural fusion. By the time of Henry VIII, it no longer made sense to speak of the people of Ireland as Celtic Norse, Norman, Welsh or English. They had merged together to become the Irish.

Until the seventeenth century AD, Celtic customs and practices lingered in isolated rural enclaves, kept alive by habit and tradition. Among those who were proud of their ancient heritage, the Celtic tongue persisted, although the words and phrases had changed greatly from the language spoken by Brigid and Columcille. And in taverns and noble halls, poets still sang songs of the heroic past, recalling brave deeds and fiery courtships. But Celtic paradigms were slowly fading, losing their separate identity and ability to influence behaviour. The emerging Irish culture eventually combined old beliefs with new viewpoints to form the complex society of modern Ireland.

In 1541, Henry VIII accelerated the process of decline for the Celtic way of life when he decided to increase his level of direct political control over Ireland. He began a series of wars with the Irish that were vigorously pursued by his successors to the English throne. The Irish who resisted the ambitions of England were forced to create a new national identity, uniting all of the inhabitants of the island under a common cultural banner. Perhaps the final blow to the lingering remnants of the

Celtic way of life came from the Puritan armies of Cromwell and Ireton with their military occupation of the entire island in 1652. Or perhaps the end came in 1691 when the Treaty of Limerick forced thousands of Irish to forever live in exile from their homeland. By the eighteenth century, the descendants of the once fiercely independent Celts lived as downtrodden tenants in their own country, uncertain of their future while glorifying their past. And in the wake of battles, famine, and land confiscation, even the new composite Irish culture had to struggle to survive. When the political, religious, and cultural hegemony of the English was complete, Irish links with its Celtic past became merely a memory kept alive by legend, folklore, and the occasional Celtic word spoken by impoverished farmers.

The Celts of Scotland and Wales fared little better. During the centuries of resistance to English political and religious control, a merger of cultures occurred similar to Ireland. In the remote highlands and western isles, Celtic customs and practices endured. But like their cousins in Ireland, any people who lived by the traditional Celtic ways were regarded as crude and unsophisticated by the English aristocracy and the evolving Scottish middle class. The modern age created new definitions of wealth and political power which consigned to poverty and obscurity any Celts who viewed the world according to outmoded paradigms.

As purely Celtic society disintegrated, its unique sexual viewpoints also vanished. The dominant institutions of government, religion, and family no longer validated traditional Celtic sexual behaviour. Instead, Irish, Scottish and Welsh society developed new models for sexuality based on a composite of Anglican, Roman Catholic and Presbyterian viewpoints. The end result was a perception of sexuality and its role in human affairs far different from the Celtic.

In the lands once ruled by the Celts, religion became the prime criterion for allocating wealth and defining national identity. The dominant Anglican Church of England did not tolerate rivals and wielded enough political power to suppress the Catholics and Presbyterians. The English and Irish Parliaments passed burdensome laws placing severe civil restrictions on Catholics to insure they would never again challenge Anglican dominance. The result was a society split not only on the basis of wealth and poverty, but also on the basis of religion. For the wretched poor of Ireland, Scotland and Wales, law was unjust, government was remote, and education was unattainable. Religion became the only viable institution in their society, the only available model to define the world and their place in it. Catholic and Presbyterian paradigms became the sole guide for the bedroom behaviour of the rural peasants and working class.

The sexuality of the Celtic people and their descendants was never isolated from the complex conditions shaping their society. The paradigms they created to govern sexual behaviour and beliefs varied over time, reflecting the changing role of sexuality for individuals and the community. Sexuality was interwoven with the political, religious and philosophic ideas defining a person's relationship with the universe. In turn, sexual behaviour influenced war and prayer and crime. Whenever new and unusual experiences challenged the basic institutions and paradigms of Celtic society, viewpoints realigned themselves. At the same time, sexual beliefs also changed. And only when the Celts merged with other peoples to become the Irish and Scots and Welsh did their unique concepts of sexuality fade.

The Celts of ancient times were little different from the men and women who walked the earth after them. When happy, they laughed. When sad, they wept. And when sexually aroused, they responded with passion. They differed from their descendants only in the means they chose to express their joy and sorrow and ardour.

The traditional Celtic beliefs about love and sexuality still survive in myth and folklore and rustic customs. The stories of men and women pursuing sexual satisfaction through indulgence, the tales of saints seeking sexual happiness through abstinence are an echo from the past exerting a subtle influence on the present. And in part, the sexuality of the ancient

Celts helps to define the views of their descendants concerning sex, love, and the relationship between the genders.

Notes

1. Sexual Transitions

1. John C. Messenger, 'Sex and Repression in an Irish Folk Community', ed. Donald Marshall and Robert Suggs, *Human Sexual Behavior* (New York: Basic Books, 1971).

2. Nicholas Cheetham, *A History of the Popes* (New York: Dorset, 1992), 5. The term 'papas' or pope was derived from the Latin word for father and was applied to the leaders of early Christan communities. It did not become the exclusive designation for the Bishop of Rome until the Middle Ages.

3. Peter Berresford Ellis, *Celt and Saxon* (London: Constable, 1993, 119-120. Although the Celtic Christians travelled frequently to Rome, they consciously chose to ignore doctrines they disagreed with.

4. Michael Oakeshott, 'The Tower of Babel', *Rationalism in Politics and Other Essays* (Indianapolis, Indiana: Liberty Press, 1991), 486.

5. Uta Ranke-Heinemann, *Eunuchs for the Kingdom of Heaven*, trans. Peter Heinegg (New York: Doubleday, 1988), 153-67.

6. Ellis, *Celt and Saxon,* 20-25.

7. Michael Richter, *Medieval Ireland: The Enduring Tradition* (Dublin: Gill and Macmillan, 1988), 129. The papal authorization for the English invasion of Ireland was issued by Adrian IV born as Nicholas Breakspear. He was the only Englishman ever elected to the papacy.

2. The Land of Innocence

1. Michael Dame, *Mythic Ireland* (London: Thames and Hudson, 1992), 34.

2. H.D. Rankin, *Celts and the Classical World* (London: Areopagitica Press, 1987), 249-50.

3. Otto Kiefer, *Sexual Life in Ancient Rome* (London: Constable, 1993), 30-39.

4. Patrick C. Power, *Sex and Marriage in Ancient Ireland* Dublin: Mercier Press, 1976: repr. 1993), 31-39.

5. Rankin, 250.

6. James Charles Roy, *Islands of Storm* (Chester Springs, Pennsylvania: Dufour Editions, 1991), 1989.

7. Christian scribes expanded the myths of Oisin the son of Finn and the children of Lir, enabling them to miraculously live long enough to become Christian.

8. Richter, 68.

9. *The Táin*, trans. Thomas Kinsella (Oxford: Oxford University Press, 1969), 27.

10. Alwyn Rees and Brinley Rees, *Celtic Heritage* (London: Thames and Hudson, 1961: repr. 1991), 104-109.

11. ibid., 106.

12. J.P. Mallory, *In Search of the Indo-Europeans* (London: Thames and Hudson, 1989), 110-111.

13. *The Táin*, 35-49.

14. ibid., 53.

15. ibid., 6-8.

16. ibid., 141.

17. ibid., 134-136.

18. T.W. Rolleston, *Celtic Myths and Legends* (London: Harrap, 1917: repr. London: Constable, 1990), 156-158.

19. Mary Condren, *The Serpent and the Goddess: Women, Religion and Power in Celtic Ireland* (San Francisco: Harper, 1989), 89.

3. Christian Sexuality

1. Brendan Lehane, *Early Celtic Christianity* (London: Constable, 1993), 24.

2. Roy, 101.

3. Peter Berresford Ellis, *Celtic Inheritance* (London: Constable, 1992), 34.

4. Aline Rousselle, *Porneia*, trans. Felicia Pheasant (Cambridge, Massachusetts: Blackwell, 1989), 5-24.

5. Ranke-Heinemann, 10-15.

6. ibid., 101-102.

7. *The Middle Ages: A Concise Encyclopedia,* trans. H.R. Loyn (London: Thames and Hudson, 1989), 217.

8. Ranke-Heinemann, 80-82.

9. Malcolm Godwin, *Angels: An Endangered Species* (New York: Simon and Schuster, 1990), 36.

10. Ambrose, *The Later Christian Fathers,* trans. and ed. Henry Bettenson (Oxford: Oxford University Press, 1972), 177-186.

11. ibid., 191-251.

12. The ecclesiastical supremacy of the Bishop of Rome was based on the 'Tu es Petrus' line of the gospel which may have been inserted in the third century and a spurious letter from Peter to the first Bishop of Rome granting him apostolic succession. The legitimacy of these claims was not recognized in the Eastern Christian Church. See Reinach, Salomon, *Orpheus* (New York: Horace Liveright, 1930), 240.

13. Ellis, *Celtic Inheritance,* 35-36.

14. Ranke-Heinemann, 123.

15. ibid., 127-128.

16. Kieffer, 1-30.

4. Pagans and Christians

1. Guy de la Bedoyere, *The Finds of Roman Britain* (London: Batsford, 1989), 182-186.

2. Ellis, *Celt and Saxon*, 119-120.

3. ibid., 121.

4. William Parker Marsh and Christopher Bamford, eds. *Celtic Christianity: Ecology and Holiness* (Hudson, New York: Lindisfarne Press, 1987), 11. Although this quote is credited to Taliesin, it does not appear in his writings.

5. ibid., 18.

6. ibid., 18-20.

7. ibid., 48.

8. John Matthews, *Taliesin: Shamanism and the Bardic Mysteries in Britain and Ireland* (London: Aquarian, 991), 155-177.

9. Ellis, *Celtic Inheritance*, 42-43.

10. Richter, 97-98.

11. Condren, 120.

12. Ellis, *Celtic Inheritance*, 44.

13. Roy, 189.

14. ibid., 184.

15. Rees, 224.

16. James Bonwick, *Irish Druids and Old Irish Religions* (New York: Dorset, 1986), 281.

17. The Venerable Bede, *Baedae Opera Historica,* vol. 1, trans. J.E. King (Cambridge, Massachusetts: Harvard University Press, 1939: repr. 1976), 460.

18. ibid., 461.

5. Mother, Lover and Hag

1. Lehane, 55.

2. Mother, lover, and hag are the three basic archetypes assigned to women in Celtic mythology and perhaps are remnant paradigms from earlier cultures: see Shirley Toulson, *The Celtic Year* (Rockport, Massachussetts: Element, 1993), 81.

3. Thomas S. Kuhn, *The Structure of Scientific Revolutions,* 2nd. ed. (Chicago: The University of Chicago Press, 1978), 43-49.

4. David A. Hollinger, 'T.S. Kuhn's Theory of Science and its Implications for History', *Paradigms and Revolutions,* ed. Gary Gutting (Notre Dame, Indiana: University of Notre Dame Press, 1980), 197.

5. ibid., 199.

6. Ellis, *Celt and Saxon*, 91.

7. Hollinger, 212-213.

6. The Saxon Catalyst

1. Bede, 71. Bede calls Horsa and Hengeist Jutes, but evidence indicates they may have been Franks. For simplicity, Angles, Jutes and Saxons will all be referred to as Saxons.

2. Graham Webster, *Boudica*, rev. ed. (London: Batsford, 1978), 30.

3. ibid., 129-130.

4. Ellis, *Celt and Saxon*, 91. See also *The Saxon Chronicle*, trans. J. Ingram (London: Studio Editions, 1993, orig. pub. 1823), 25-49 for the Saxon account of the slaughtering of the Celts.

5. ibid., 52.

6. ibid., 137.

7. *Beowulf*, trans. Crossley-Holland (n.p.: Phoebe Phillips Editions, 1987), 17.

8. Ellis, *Celt and Saxon*, 54.

9. *Beowulf*, 83.

10. The Celtic colony of Armorica (now Brittany) endured and the language still spoken there is a Celtic dialect called Breton.

11. Richter, 28-29.

12. Some modern English historians tend to discount the writings of Gildas, opting for a gradual assimilation theory that portrays the Saxons as less brutal. See Nora K. Chadwick, *Celt and Saxon – Studies in Early English Borders* (Cambridge: Cambridge University Press, 1963)

13. Wayne A. Meeks, *The Origins of Christian Morality: The First Two Centuries* (New Haven, Connecticut: Yale University Press, 1993), 18. The failure of a major societal institution causes people to question all other institutions.

14. Kuhn, 93.

15. Bede, 71.

16. Meeks, 85.

17. Richter, 5. While it is impossible to know the exact demographic distribution of Christians in Britain and Ireland during the sixth century AD, the geographic distribution of monasteries provides a clue.

18. Meeks, 55.

19. ibid., 53-54.

20. ibid., 21.

21. Reay Tannahill, *Sex in History* (n.p.: Stein and Day, 1980. rev. ed. Scarborough, 1992), 137.

7. Spiritual Warriors

1. Barrie Ruth Strauss, *The Catholic Church* (New York: Hippocrene, 1992), 30-35.

2. Ranke-Heinemann, 81.

3. Samuel Hugh Moffett, A *History of Christianity in Asia,* vol.1 (San Francisco: Harper, 1992), 77. The Syrian ascetic movement had a greater focus on community involvement than the Egyptian.

4. Lehane, 14.

5. Roy, 84.

6. Rousselle, 143.

7. Simeon the Stylite shackled himself with weights and spent long days atop high pillars. He became quite a tourist attraction and perhaps enjoyed the notoriety.

8. Roy, 83-84.

9. Rousselle, 160-161

10. Roy, 90.

11. Eusebius, *A History of the Church from Christ to Constantine,* trans. G.A. Williamson (New York: Barnes and Noble, 1965), 247-248. Although Origen's act received official Christian disapproval, he was praised for his enthusiasm and the genuineness of his faith.

12. Origen, *The Early Christian Fathers,* trans. and ed., Henry Bettenson (Oxford: Oxford University Press, 1969), 269.

13. Rousselle, 143.

14. Ellis, *Celtic Inheritance*, 30.

15. Bettenson, 6.

16. Roy, 128.

17. Braunfels, Wolfgang, *Monasteries of Western Europe: The Architecture of the Orders* (New York: Thames and Hudson, 1972), 20.

18. Ellis, *Celtic Inheritance*, 30.

19. Roy, 126.

20. Rousselle, 153.

21. Foucault, Michael, 'The Battle for Chastity', *Western Sexuality,* eds. P. Aries and A. Beigin (London: Blackwell, 1985), 172.

22. Meeks, 54.

23. Rousselle, 151.

24. ibid., 164-166.

25. ibid., 141-148.

26. ibid., 152.

27. Braunfels, 232-233.

28. Rousselle, 155.

29. ibid., 170.

30. Foucault, 173.

31. Both John Chrysostum and Tertullian believed that the knowledge of sexual pleasure made celibacy very difficult for women. They advocated the isolation of widows so they would not taint virgin women with stories of their sexual experience.

32. Roy, 131.

33. James, Simon, *The World of the Celts* (London: Thames and Hudson, 1993), 91.

34. Matthews, Caitlin, *The Elements of the Celtic Tradition* (Rockport, Massachusetts: Element, 1989), 57-62.

35. Richter, 69-70.

36. Ellis, *Celtic Inheritance*, 39.

37. Braunfels, 24.

8. Columcille

1. Roy, 17.

2. Lehane, 118.

3. Ellis, *Celtic Inheritance,* 86.

4. Seamus MacManus, *The Story of the Irish Race,* rev. ed. (Old Greenwich, Connecticut: Devon-Adair, 1921), 163.

5. Roy, 18.

6. Lehane, 118-119.

7. Roy, 19.

8. Ellis, *Celtic Inheritance,* 87.

9. A distinction also existed between the Red Christ, emphasizing his suffering and death, and the White Christ, emphasizing his spirituality.

10. Ellis, *Celtic Inheritance,* 84.

11. Bonwick, 282.

12. Lehane, 121.

13. Roy, 145.

14. Ellis, *Celtic Inheritance,* 111.

15. Padraic Colum, ed. *A Treasury of Irish Folklore,* 2nd. rev. ed. (London: Crown, 1954: New York: Wing, 1992), 127-128.

16. Lehane, 132.

17. Colum, 129.

18. Lehane, 133.

19. Lady Gregory, *The Blessed Trinity of Ireland* (Gerard's Cross, England: Colin Smythe, 1985), 34-35.

20. The abbots of Iona crowned the Scottish kings on the *Lia Fail,* a sacred stone reputedly brought to Ireland by the Tuatha dé Danaan. The stone is now housed in Westminster. The abbots also buried the kings at Iona. Shakespeare refers to this in *Macbeth* when Ross asks about the disposition of Duncan's body. Macduff replies 'Carried to Colme-kill, The sacred storehouse of his predecessors, And guardian of their bones.' *Macbeth,* II(ii).

9. Columbanus

1. Lehane, 147.

2. Ellis, *Celtic Inheritance,* 133.

3. Richter, 57.

4. Fr. Funck-Bretano, *A History of Gaul: Celtic, Roman and Frankish Rule,* trans. E.F. Buckley (New York: Barnes & Noble, 1993).

5. Lehane, 150.

6. Funck-Bretano, 264. Contains a synopsis of the dynastic struggles between the partition of 567 AD and the arrival of Columbanus.

7. Lehane, 130-134.

8. ibid., 158-59.

9. Funck-Bretano, 264. Gregory of Tous described Brunhilde as a virtuous woman, praising her generosity to the Christian Church.

10. In fairness to Brunhilde, she was a capable administrator who instituted land reform and curtailed the excesses of the bishops and nobles.

11. Toulson, 40.

12. Lehane, 158-159.

13. Jacob Streit, *Sun and Cross,* trans. Hugh Latham (Edinbugh: Floris Books, 1993), 189-190.

14. Richter, 76. The Penitential of Columbanus emphasized physical chastisement to a higher degree than other penitentials.

15. Streit, 190.

16. Funck-Bretano, 280. Roman Christian bishops controlled the cities and the surrounding lands, often wielding more power than dukes.

17. Lehane, 166-169.

18. ibid., 167.

19. Ellis, *Celtic Inheritance,* 134. Columbanus admitted that the Bishop of Rome could determine acceptable Christian ritual in certain circumstances. See also, Bede, 221. Bishop Laurentis cites Columbanus' acceptance of the Roman Easter calculation in a letter sent to Irish bishops.

20. Funck-Bretano, 252. Polygamy and concubinage were accepted practices in the Frankish royal houses.

21. Kiefer, 39.

22. Chlotar eventually executed Brunhilde in 613 AD.

23. Marsh, 124.

24. Lehane, 149.

25. Meeks, 101-102.

10. The Cult of The Virgin Mary

1. Condren, 163.

2. Meeks, 54.

3. Ranke-Heinemann, 31.

4. ibid., 343.

5. Condren, 160.

6. Marija Gambutas, *The Civilization of the Goddess* (San Francisco: Harper, 1991), 248.

7. Condren, 161.

8. Ellis, 191-192.

9. Lehane, 105.

10. Lloyd Laing and Jenifer Laing, *Art of the Celts* (London: Thames and Hudson, 1992), 175-176.

11. Condren, 162.

11. Brigid of Kildare

1. The Life of Brigid by Cogitus was probably the first of the Celtic Lives of the Saints composed in the late sixth century.

2. Peter Berresford Ellis, *Dictionary of Irish Mythology* (Oxford: Oxford University Press, 1991), 50.

3. James, 115. There was no evidence that the Celts differentiated labour between the genders in a manner similar to Roman society.

4. Rankin, 132.

5. James, 129.

6. Gregory, 9. Legend claimed that Brigid was baptized by angels.

7. Marsh, 64.

8. ibid., 65.

9. ibid., 66.

10. *The Táin,* 12-20.

11. Proincias Mac Cana, *Celtic Mythology,* rev. ed. (New York: Hammlyn, 1983), 34.

12. Condren, 70-71.

13. Bonwick, 201.

14. Barbara G. Walker, *The Woman's Dictionary of Symbols and Sacred Objects* (San Francisco: Harper, 1988), 226.

15. At one time the Vestal Virgins may have been the harem of the Roman kings on whom they fathered their successors. Virginity was later introduced to limit the number of claimants to the throne. See Robert Graves, *The White Goddess,* amend. ed. (New York: Farrar, Straus and Giroux, 1948) 357-359.

16. Walker, 102.

17. Mallory, 18.

18. Condren, 71.

19. Vern Bullough and Bonni Bullough, *Sin, Sickness and Sanity: A History of Sexual Attitudes* (New York: New American Library, 1977), 77.

20. Brigid was not the only woman bishop. Beverly, the disciple of the Abbess Hilda, was also reputed to have been a bishop.

21. Oakeshott, 486.

22. ibid., 471.

12. Power and Sexuality

1. Meeks, 111-113.

2. ibid., 115-116.

3. Matthew 10:1.

4. Matthew 10:34-37.

5. 'Tu es Petris' was not used as a basis for papal authority until the time of Damasius I, Bishop of Rome, 366-384 AD.

6. 'England' refers to the part of Britain occupied by Angles, Saxons and Jutes.

7. Cheetham, 43.

8. Bede, 211.

9. ibid., 203.

10. *The Saxon Chronicle*, 18 indicates the West Saxon king Cynegils became a Christian between 560 AD and 590 AD, probably from Celtic influence.

11. Roy, 196.

12. Strauss, 57.

13. Cheetham, 38-39.

14. ibid., 40

15. Bede, 111. As part of the marriage contract with Ethelbert, Bertha was guaranteed free practice of the Christian religion.

16. ibid., 121.

17. Cheetham, 41.

18. Bede, 141.

19. ibid., 121.

20. ibid., 211. A Celtic military defeat a few years later was deemed to fulfil Augustine's prophecy.

21. Ellis, *Celt and Saxon,* 78-79.

22. ibid., 143.

23. Bede, 337.

24. ibid, 315-321. When Edwin controlled the throne, the Roman priest Paulinus was attached to his court. Paulinus abandoned Northumbria when Edwin was deposed.

25. ibid., 461.

26. Matthew 16:18. The passage also implies that the forces of evil will try to prevail against the inheritors of Peter's authority.

27. Bede, 477.

28. Ellis, *Celtic Inheritance,* 123.

29. 1 Thessalonians 4.

30. Funck-Bretano, 230. Clotilda may have been the second wife of Clovis in a polygamous relationship. He was married before and it is unclear if he was a widower, divorced, or had several wives.

31. Cheetham, 43.

32. Bede, 249.

33. ibid., 263-269.

13. Crime and Sexuality

1. Ellis, *Celtic Inheritance*, 16.

2. MacManus, 132.

3. Richter, 88.

4. Nora K. Chadwick, *The Celts* (London: Pelican, 1971: repr. Penguin, 1991), 117.

5. Power, 9.

6. ibid., 14.

7. ibid., 19.

8. ibid., 30.

9. ibid., 46

10. ibid., 26.

11. J.M. Kelly, A *Short History of Western Legal Theory* (Oxford: Clarendon Press, 1992), 89.

12. Condren, 88-89.

13. Power, 64.

14. Condren, 91.

15. Andrew McCall, *The Medieval Underworld* (Dorset Press: New York, 1979), 202-16

16. Bede, 281.

17. Even the prototypical male warrior CúChúlain had to bargain for Aife's sexual services after defeating her in combat.

18. Condren, 54.

19. Richter, 94.

20. ibid., 127.

21. ibid., 90.

14. Invasions, Brothels and Witches

1. Richard Roche, *The Norman Invasion of Ireland* (Dublin: Anvil Books, 1970), 32.

2. MacManus, 332.

3. Richter, 131.

4. Theodore F.T. Plucknett, A *Concise History of The Common Law* (Boston: Little Brown & Co., 1956), 528-529.

5. MacManus, 338.

6. McCall, 182-183.

7. During the late Medieval period, a lease created an estate in land similar to a temporary sale. The owner of the land was not responsible for any of the activities of the lessee provided the land was returned in the original condition at the end of the lease.

8. McCall, 184.

9. Lujo Basserman, *The Oldest Profession: A History of Prostitution*, trans. James Cleugh (New York: Dorset, 1993), 83.

10. ibid., ff. 83.

11. R. Gillespie, 'Women and Crime in Seventeenth Century Ireland', ed. Margaret MacCurtain and Mary ó Dowd, *Women in Early Modern Ireland* (Dublin: Wolfhound Press, 1991), 50.

12. Ranke-Heinemann, 179.

13. Fredrich Heer, *The Medieval World*, trans. Janet Sondheimer (New York: Mentor, 1962), 317-323.

14. St. John D. Seymour, *Irish Witchcraft and Demonology* (New York: Dorset, 1992), 47.

15. ibid., 44. John XXII had a pathological fear that witches were plying their magical arts to harm him, perhaps accounting for his sponsorship of witch persecution throughout Europe.

16. ibid., 27-28.

17. Richter, 166-167.

Bibliography

Bamford, Christopher, and William Paker Marsh. *Celtic Christianity Ecology and Holiness*. Hudson, New York: Lindisfarne Press, 1982.

Barbour, Ian. 'Paradigms in Science and Religion', *Paradigms and Revolutions*. ed. Gary Gutting. Notre Dame, Indiana: University of Notre Dame Press, 1980.

Basserman, Lujo. *The Oldest Profession: A History of Prostitution*. trans. James Cleugh. New York: Dorsett, 1993.

Bede. *Opera Historica*. trans. J.E. King. 2 vols. Cambridge, Massachusetts: Harvard University Press, 1930.

Beowulf. trans. Kevin Crossley-Holland. N.P.: Phoebe Phillips Editions, 1987.

Bettenson, Henry, ed. and trans. *The Early Christian Fathers*. 2 vols. Oxford: Oxford University Press, 1956.

Bonwick, James. *Irish Druids and Old Irish Religions*. New York: Dorsett, 1986.

Braunfels, Wolfgang. *The Architecture of the Monasteries of Western Europe*. trans. Alistair Liang. London: Thames and Hudson, 1972.

Bullough, Vern, and Bonnie Bullough. *Sin, Sex and Sanity: A History of Sexual Attitudes*. New York: New American Library, 1977.

Chadwick, Nora K. *Celt and Saxon – Studies in Early English Borders*. Cambridge: Cambridge University Press, 1963.

——— *The Celts*. London: Pelican, 1971, repr. London: Penguin, 1991.

Cheetham, Nicholas. A *History of the Popes*. New York. Dorset, 1992.

Colum, Padraig. *A Treasury of Irish Folklore*. New York: rev. ed. Wings Books, 1992.

Condren, Mary. *The Serpent and The Goddess*. San Francisco: Harper, 1989.

Dames, Michael. *Mythic Ireland*. London: Thames and Hudson, 1992.

de la Bedoyere, Guy. *The Finds of Roman Britain*. London: B.T. Batsford Ltd., 1989.

de Lubac, Henri. *The Eternal Feminine*. trans. Rene Hague. London: Collins, 1971.

Ellis, Peter Berresford. *Celt and Saxon*. London: Constable, 1993.

——— *The Celtic Empire*. London: Constable, 1990.

——— *Celtic Inheritance*. London: Constable, 1992.

——— *A Dictionary of Irish Mythology*. Oxford. Oxford University Press, 1991.

Eusebius. *The History of the Church.* trans. G.A. Williamson. New York: Dorset, 1984.

Foucault, Michael. 'The Battle for Chastity'. *Western Sexuality.* eds. P. Aries and A. Bejin. Oxford: Basil Blackwell Ltd., 1985.

Funck-Brentano, Fr. *A History of Gaul: Celtic, Roman and Frankish Rule.* trans. E.F. Buckley. New York: Barnes and Noble, 1993.

Gambutas, Marija. *The Civilization of the Goddess.* San Francisco: Harper, 1991.

Gildas. *The Ruin of Britain and Other Works.* ed. and trans. Michael Winterbottom. London: Philmore, 1978.

Gillespie, R. 'Women and Crime in Seventeenth Century Ireland'. *Women in Early Modern Ireland.* eds. Margaret MacCurtain and Mary O'Dowd. Dublin: Wolfhound Press, 1991.

Godwin, Malcolm. *Angels.* New York: Simon and Shuster, 1990.

Graves, Robert. *The White Goddess.* New York: Farrar, Straus and Giroux, 1948.

Gregory, Lady. *The Blessed Trinity of Ireland.* Gerards Cross, England: Colin Smyth, 1985.

Heer, Frederich. *The Medieval World.* trans. Janet Sondheimer. New York: Mentor, 1962.

Hollinger, David A. 'T.S. Kuhn's Theory of Science and its Implications for History.' *Paradigms and Revolutions.* ed. Gary Gutting. Notre Dame, Indiana: University of Notre Dame Press, 1980.

Hubert, Henri. *The History of the Celtic People.* London: Bracken Books, orig. pub. 1934, repr. 1992.

James, Simon. *The World of the Celts.* London: Thames and Hudson, 1993.

Kelly, J.M. *A Short History of Western Legal Theory.* Oxford: Clarendon Press, 1992.

Kiefer, Otto. *Sexual Life in Ancient Rome.* London: Constable, 1993.

Kuhn, Thomas S. *The Structure of Scientific Revolutions.* Chicago: University of Chicago Press, 2nd. ed., 1970.

Laing, Lloyd and Jennifer Laing. *Art of the Celts.* London: Thames and Hudson, 1992.

Lehane, Brendan. *Early Celtic Christianity.* London: Constable, 1993.

MacManus, Seumas. *The Story of the Irish Race.* Old Greenwich, Connecticut: The Devin-Adair Co., 1921.

Mallory, J.P. *In Search of the Indo-Europeans.* London: Thames and Hudson, 1989.

Matthews, Caitlin. *The Elements of the Celtic Tradition.* Rockport, Massachusetts: Element, 1989.

Matthews, John. *Taliesin: Shamanism and the Bardic Mysteries in Britain and Ireland.* The Aquarian Press: London, 1991.

MacCana, Proinsias. *Celtic Mythology.* New York: Hammlyn, 1968, rev. ed. 1983.

McCall, Andrew. *The Medieval Underworld.* New York: Dorset, 1979.

Meeks, Wayne A. *The Origins of Christian Morality: The First Two Centuries.* New Haven, Connecticut: Yale University Press, 1993.

Messenger, John C. 'Sex and Repression in an Irish Folk Community'. *Human Sexual Behavior.* eds. Donald Marshall and Robert Suggs. New York: Basic Books. 1971.

Moffett, Samuel Hugh. A *History of Christianity in Asia*. Vol. 1. San Francisco: Harper, 1992.

Oakeshott, Michael. 'The Tower of Babel'. *Rationalism in Politics and Other Essays*. Indianapolis, Indiana: Liberty Press, 1991.

ó Cathasaigh, Donal. 'The Cult of Bridgid'. *Mother Worship*. ed. J. Preston. Chapel Hill, North Carolina: The University of North Carolina Press, 1982.

ó Corráin, Donnchadh and Fildema Maguire. *Irish Names*. Dublin: Lilliput Press, 1981.

Plucknett, Theodore F.Y. *A Concise History of the Common Law*. Boston: Little Brown and Co., 1956.

Power, Patrick C. *Sex and Marriage in Ancient Ireland*. Dublin: Mercier Press, 1976.

——— *The Book of Irish Curses*. Dublin: Mercier Press, 1974.

Ranke-Heinemann, Uta. *Eunuchs for the Kingdom of Heaven*. New York: Doubleday, 1990.

Ranken, H.D. *Celts and the Classical World*. London: Areopagitica Press, 1987.

Reinach, Salomon. *Orpheus*. New York: Horace Liveright, 1930.

Richter, Michael. *Medieval Ireland: The Enduring Tradition*. Dublin: Gill and Macmillan, Ltd., 1983.

Rees, Alwyn and Brinley Rees. *Celtic Heritage*. London: Thames and Hudson, 1961.

Roche, Richard. *The Norman Invasion of Ireland*. Dublin: Anvil Books, 1970.

Rolleston, T.W. *Celtic Myths and Legends*. London: Constable, orig. pub. 1911, repr. 1990.

Rouselle, Aline. *Porneia*. trans. Felicia Pheasant. Cambridge, Massachusetts: Blackwell, 1988.

Roy, James Charles. *Islands of Storm*. Chester Springs, Pennsylvania: Dufour Editions, 1991.

The Saxon Chronicle. trans. J. Ingraham. London: orig. pub. 1823, Studio Editions, 1993.

Seymour, St. John D. *Irish Witchcraft and Demonology*. New York: Dorset, 1992.

Shapere, Dudly. 'The Structure of Scientific Revolutions'. *Paradigms and Revolutions*. ed. Gary Gutting. Notre Dame, Indiana: University of Notre Dame Press, 1980.

Sjoo, Monica and Barbara Mor. *The Great Cosmic Mother*. San Francisco: Harper and Row, 1975.

Spence, Lewis. *The Magic Arts in Celtic Britain*. New York: Dorset, 1992.

Strauss, Barrie Ruth. *The Catholic Church*. New York: Hippocrene Books, 1992.

Streit, Jakob. *Sun and Cross*. trans. Hugh Latham. Edinburgh, U.K.: Floris Books, 1984.

Táin Bó Cualinge. trans. Thomas Kinsella. Oxford: Oxford University Press, 1969.

Tannahill, Reay. *Sex in History*. N.P.: rev. ed., Scarborough House, 1992.

Taylor, G. Rattray. *Sex in History*. New York: Thames and Hudson, 1954.

Toulson, Shirley. *The Celtic Year*. Rockport, Massachusetts: Element, 1993.

Walker, Barbara G. *The Woman's Dictionary of Symbols and Sacred Objects*. San Francisco: Harper, 1988.

Webster, Graham. *Boudica*. London: B.T. Batsford, orig. pub. 1978, rev. ed. 1993.

Wentz, W.Y. Evans. *The Fairy Faith in Celtic Countries*. Gerards Cross, U.K.: orig. pub. Oxford University Press. 1911, repr. Colin Smyth Ltd., 1977.

Index